Success in Writing

Writing to Explain

GLOBE FEARON
EDUCATIONAL PUBLISHER
A Division of Simon & Schuster
Upper Saddle River, New Jersey

Executive Editor: Barbara Levadi
Senior Editor: Francie Holder
Project Editors: Karen Bernhaut, Douglas Falk, Amy Jolin
Editorial Assistant: Kris Shepos-Salvatore
Editorial Development: Kraft & Kraft
Production Director: Penny Gibson
Production Editor: Alan Dalgleish
Interior Design and Electronic Page Production: Blue Inc.
Marketing Manager: Nancy Surridge
Cover Design: Leslie Baker, Pat Smythe

Printed in the United States of America
3 4 5 6 7 8 9 10   99 98

ISBN 0-835-91890-4

GLOBE FEARON EDUCATIONAL PUBLISHER
A Division of Simon & Schuster
Upper Saddle River, New Jersey

CONTENTS

UNIT 1 Understanding Exposition.. 5

Chapter 1 Building an Explanation 6

   Lesson 1 Beginning with the Introduction 7

   Lesson 2 Writing a Thesis Statement............................... 8

   Lesson 3 Explaining with a Purpose 9

   Lesson 4 Getting Organized 10

   Lesson 5 Ending with a Conclusion 12

Chapter 2 Explaining with Style.................................. 13

   Lesson 1 Using Transitions 14

   Lesson 2 Adding Details 16

What Have You Learned in Unit 1? 17

UNIT 2 Writing to Explain 18

Chapter 1 Planning Your Writing 19

   Lesson 1 Choosing a Topic 20

   Lesson 2 Narrowing a Topic 21

   Lesson 3 Identifying the Audience 23

   Lesson 4 Identifying the Purpose 24

   Lesson 5 Gathering Information................................... 25

   Lesson 6 Organizing Information................................. 26

Chapter 2 Developing Your Writing............................. 28

   Lesson 1 Drafting the Introduction 29

   Lesson 2 Drafting the Body....................................... 30

   Lesson 3 Drafting the Conclusion................................ 32

Chapter 3 Completing Your Writing 33

   Lesson 1 Revising Your Essay 34

   Lesson 2 Proofreading Your Essay 36

   Lesson 3 Publishing Your Essay 37

What Have You Learned in Unit 2?............................ 38

UNIT 3 Writing on Your Own **39**

Chapter 1 Summarizing a Story **40**

   Lesson 1 Mapping a Story **41**

   Lesson 2 Drafting Your Summary **43**

   Lesson 3 Completing Your Summary **45**

Chapter 2 Writing a How-to Explanation **47**

   Lesson 1 Deciding What the Audience Needs **48**

   Lesson 2 Organizing by Sequence **50**

   Lesson 3 Drafting Your How-to Explanation **52**

   Lesson 4 Completing Your How-to Explanation ... **53**

Chapter 3 Comparing and Contrasting **54**

   Lesson 1 Selecting Important Details **55**

   Lesson 2 Organizing Information **57**

   Lesson 3 Drafting Your Essay **58**

   Lesson 4 Completing Your Essay **59**

What Have You Learned in Unit 3? **60**

UNIT 4 Writing on Assignment **61**

Chapter 1 Writing a Test Essay **62**

   Lesson 1 Understanding the Prompt **64**

   Lesson 2 Organizing Your Thoughts Quickly **65**

   Lesson 3 Drafting Under a Deadline **66**

   Lesson 4 Completing a Test Essay **68**

Chapter 2 Writing a Research Report **69**

   Lesson 1 Gathering Information **70**

   Lesson 2 Taking Notes **71**

   Lesson 3 Organizing Your Report **72**

   Lesson 4 Writing Your Report **73**

What Have You Learned in Unit 4? **74**

The Writing Process **75**

A Guide for Writers: Grammar, Mechanics, and Usage **76**

UNIT 1 Understanding Exposition

Expository writing is writing that explains or informs. Every time you give directions, explain a process, or define something, you are using exposition. Writing exposition is like being a teacher. Your goal is to make readers understand something that is difficult, unclear, or unfamiliar.

What to Do

Learn the purposes of different types of expository writing. Here are some of their purposes:

- to define a term
- to summarize a book or article
- to compare and contrast two people, places, or ideas
- to tell how to solve a problem
- to explain how to do something
- to explain the cause of an event
- to interpret a work of literature

How to Do It

When you write an expository essay, try to make learning meaningful for your readers. Think of ways that make learning meaningful for you. Then use them in your own writing.

- Know your topic.
- Use examples and facts that support your ideas.
- Present your ideas in a clear, organized way.
- Add details to make your explanation interesting.

Apply It

▶ Make a list of topics you would like to explore in an essay of your own. Would you like to explain how something works? Would you like to write about why an event was important? Would you like to solve a problem? Jot down some notes. Keep your ideas in your notebook.

CHAPTER 1 Building an Explanation

Explaining is something that we do all our lives. It is the way we learn and the way we let others know our thoughts. This is what expository writing is all about.

What to Do Give your writing a strong structure. Your explanation might take different forms depending on your purpose. It might, for example, be a summary, a how-to explanation, a comparison-and-contrast essay, or a research paper. Whatever its form, begin with an introduction, include a main idea or thesis statement, organize your facts, and then conclude.

How to Do It Keep this chart in mind when you work on each of the three parts of an explanation.

INTRODUCTION
(1 paragraph)
Grab your reader's attention.
Make your topic and purpose clear.
State your thesis or main idea.

BODY
(1 or more paragraphs)
Support your thesis or develop your main idea.
Fit your style to your purpose.
Organize your material logically.

CONCLUSION
(1 paragraph)
Pull all of your main points together.
Summarize your thesis or main idea.

Review It **1.** What are the three main parts of an expository essay?

_____

_____

_____

2. What is one important goal to accomplish in the body of an expository essay?

_____

Lesson 1   Beginning with the Introduction

The introduction to an expository essay should make your topic and your purpose clear. Readers should know right away what you are going to explain and how you are going to explain it.

What to Do

Get your readers interested. A good introduction grabs the readers' attention. Here are some tips that can help you write an attention-grabbing introduction.

Strategies to Introduce an Expository Essay:

- Tell an anecdote. (An anecdote is a very short story.)
- Ask a question.
- State an opinion about your topic.
- Give a startling or surprising fact.
- Quote someone.

How to Do It

Look at this example. It comes from a research paper Vernon was assigned to write. He chose to write about the student protests during the Vietnam War. Here is the introduction to his essay.

> "At the time, I wasn't quite sure myself why we were protesting. I did ask myself some questions. Were we afraid of going to war? Did we know for sure that the Vietnam War was wrong? Maybe it was a little of both. For sure, though, some kids were just following the crowd." These are the words of a former student protester. They describe some of the causes of student protests against the Vietnam War in the late 1960s and early 1970s. There were other causes that led to those protests as well.

Review It

1. Do you think the quoted remark grabs readers' attention? Why or why not?

_____

_____

2. What other strategy could Vernon have used to start his essay?

_____

_____

Lesson 2 Writing a Thesis Statement

An expository essay makes a point. This point is called a thesis statement. A sentence in the introduction should be the thesis statement.

What to Do

Decide what point you want your essay to make. Express the main idea or thesis in a one-sentence thesis statement. Include this statement in your introduction.

Imagine that you are going to explain how to make pizza. You think that making pizza can be an adventure beyond tomato sauce and cheese. You can make that point in a thesis statement.

How to Do It

Look at this example. Yori wrote an essay explaining the importance of math in daily life. He wanted to make a point. Here is the beginning of his essay:

> Many students do not believe that math is related to their lives outside the classroom. If people would stop and think, they would recognize that they use math skills all the time. For example, my friend Tina wanted to go out for pizza and a movie with her friends last Saturday night. She had three dollars and needed at least fifteen for the evening. She also owed her sister five dollars. Tina used math skills to see how much money she needed.

Review It

1. What sentence states Yori's main idea or thesis? Copy it below.

_____

_____

2. What do you think Yori will explain next?

_____

3. Why do you think so?

_____

Lesson 3 Explaining with a Purpose

You often make decisions about what type of writing you will do. You choose a different type of writing for journal entries, reports, letters to friends, and thank-you notes. If you know your purpose and your topic for an expository essay, you can figure out what type of essay to write.

What to Do

Think about your purpose. It will lead you to the best type of expository writing for your essay.

How to Do It

This chart will help you choose the best type of writing for your purpose.

IF YOUR PURPOSE IS TO . . .	THEN YOU MIGHT WRITE . . .
tell what a book is about	a summary
show how to solve a math problem	a how-to explanation
compare two people, places, or things	a comparison-contrast essay
answer a question about a topic in science	a cause-and-effect essay
discover information about a topic that interests you	a research report

Review It

▶ Teachers sometimes ask students for brief descriptions of the essays that they plan to write for class. Read these descriptions. On the line below each one, name the type of expository essay the student will probably write.

1. I want to tell how television was invented and how it changed people's lives.

_____

2. I would like to write about Sandra Cisneros and Gary Soto. They are both writers.

_____

3. I will write an essay about hurricanes. I will tell how they form and why they are so dangerous.

_____

4. I want to sum up the story that Maya Angelou told in *I Know Why the Caged Bird Sings*.

_____

Lesson 4 Getting Organized

You should organize the body of your essay in a way that suits the topic and the purpose.

What to Do

Look at the following chart. It explains some ways that you can order details in the body of an expository essay.

ORDER	DESCRIPTION	PURPOSES
Chronological Order	Details and events are put in the order they happen.	to show how to do something to show causes and effects to summarize a story
Order of Importance	Details are arranged from the least important to the most important, or from the most important to the least important.	to help readers see how important an idea is
Point by Point	A detail about one item is given. Then a detail about a second item is given.	to compare two items to contrast two items
Subject by Subject	All the details about one item are given. Then all the details about the second item are given.	to compare two items to contrast two items
Main Idea and Details	An important idea is followed by facts, reasons, and anecdotes.	to define a term or idea to summarize nonfiction

How to Do It

Here is part of the body of an essay a student named Karla wrote for a science test.

> Most people think of big and noisy things when they think of machines. Certainly, there are machines that look as if they could take over the world. Yet, no matter how complicated a machine looks, it is based on one of the six types of simple machines. They are the lever, the wheel and axle, the pulley, the inclined plane, the wedge, and the screw. Each of these simple machines does its work in its own way.
>
> The lever is one of the simplest machines. A shovel is an example of a lever. The three things that make a lever work are the load, effort or force, and the fulcrum. The fulcrum is the pivotal, or central, point.

Review It

1. How did Karla organize the details of her essay?

_____

2. Would another method of organization have worked as well? Explain your answer.

_____

3. What do you think Karla will write about next?

_____

4. Why do you think that?

_____

Apply It

▶ Here is a copy of an essay test. On the lines following each essay question, tell how you would order details for your answer. Explain why you chose that order.

1. Compare and contrast the main characters in two short stories that you read in English class this year.

_____

_____

2. Explain why the school basketball team, which finished in first place last year, finished in last place this year.

_____

_____

3. Define the scientific term <u>photosynthesis.</u>

_____

_____

4. Explain why people should be working to protect the earth's water supply.

_____

_____

Lesson 5   Ending with a Conclusion

A conclusion will pull all of the main points of your essay together. A good conclusion helps readers understand the information you have given. It can also make your readers think more about your topic.

What to Do

Just as there are many ways to start an expository essay, there are many ways to end one. Here are some strategies you can use to write a conclusion.

Strategies to Conclude an Expository Essay:
- Summarize the main points.
- Restate your main idea or thesis.
- Give readers a new idea to think about.
- Predict something.
- Ask a question about your main idea or thesis.
- Tell a brief story to illustrate your main idea or thesis.

How to Do It

The way you conclude your essay will depend on your topic and your purpose. As part of an English test, Paulo compared and contrasted the way two poets described fog. In his introduction, he said that T. S. Eliot's description was better. Here is his conclusion:

> Although both poets use the image of a cat as a metaphor for fog, I prefer T. S. Eliot's poem over Carl Sandburg's. Eliot uses more details that help create feelings and thoughts about fog.

Review It

1. Which strategy did Paulo use to conclude his essay?

_____

2. What other strategy might Paulo have used to conclude his essay?

_____

3. Try rewriting Paulo's conclusion, using this strategy.

_____

_____

_____

_____

CHAPTER 2 Explaining with Style

Smooth transitions and vivid details will help make your explanations clear and interesting. Transitions build bridges between ideas. Details about your ideas will give your explanations a lively touch.

What to Do

Explain with style to make your writing clear. In this chapter you will explore two ways to do this.

- Using transitions.
- Adding details.

How to Do It

To make sure that your readers see connections from one idea to the next, use transitions, such as *before, then, like,* and *for example*.

WITHOUT TRANSITIONS

He started high school in Galesburg, Illinois. His family moved. He finished high school in Chicago.

WITH TRANSITIONS

In 1992, he started high school in Galesburg, Illinois. When he was sixteen, his family moved, and he finished high school in Chicago.

Add vivid details to make your explanations clear and interesting.

WITHOUT DETAILS

The killer whale is the largest sea animal. Adults are big and heavy. They look interesting.

WITH DETAILS

The killer whale is the largest sea animal. Adults can be as long as thirty feet and weigh as much as nine thousand pounds. They have a shiny black surface with a white belly.

Apply It

▶ Find examples of different expository styles. You might try newspapers, magazines, or how-to books, such as cookbooks. Notice the way the writers make clear transitions and how they use details. If you can, discuss the examples with a partner.

Lesson 1   Using Transitions

When you write an explanation, make the organization clear to your readers.

What to Do   One way to make the organization of your essay clear is to use transitions. Transitions are words and phrases that show how your ideas are related to one another. They keep ideas flowing smoothly between sentences and paragraphs.

Here is a list of transitional words and phrases to use in expository essays. The list also shows when to use these transitions.

TO SHOW TIME ORDER:	**TO SHOW ORDER OF IMPORTANCE:**
before	first
after	second
then	last
when	more important
TO SHOW HOW THINGS ARE ALIKE AND DIFFERENT:	**TO SHOW CAUSE AND EFFECT:**
like	because
unlike	therefore
on the one hand	so
nevertheless	as a result
TO ADD INFORMATION:	**TO GIVE AN EXAMPLE:**
and	for example
also	such as
furthermore	along with
moreover	for instance

How to Do It

Look at this paragraph from an essay written by a student named Elena. She wrote about how to respond to certain emergencies. Notice the way she used transitions to connect one idea to another.

Knowing what to do in an emergency can save a life. If someone is bitten by a poisonous snake, you must act quickly. The first thing to do is to take the person to the closest hospital or doctor's office. Second, try to keep the victim still. This is important because movement will make the poison spread through the body more quickly. Therefore, you should try to cut off the spread of the poison to the heart.

Review It

1. Find three transitional words or phrases that Elena uses. Write each one on a line below.

_____

_____

_____

2. Add at least one transitional word or phrase to each section of the chart on page 14.

Apply It

▶ Rewrite each of the following groups of sentences, using transitions to connect ideas.

1. Only two people registered for the class. The class was canceled.

_____

_____

2. Glacier National Park was established in 1910. It is in Montana.

_____

_____

3. Jason decided to go hiking. He had never been hiking before. He sent away for literature. He planned his trip carefully.

_____

_____

Lesson 2 Adding Details

A good essay has many details. These details enrich the essay and make it complete. Details have many purposes. They support your ideas, show how ideas are linked, provide examples, and show steps in a process.

What to Do

Use details that suit your essay. This chart shows different kinds of details that you can use.

FACTS	These are details that can be proven. They add information.
ANECDOTES	These are brief stories that tell about something funny or interesting.
EXAMPLES	These details make your meaning clear by giving specific cases.
QUOTATIONS	These details show the exact words of someone. They give your essay an expert touch.
EXPLANATION OR DEFINITION	These details improve understanding. They add information.

How to Do It

Dan wrote an essay about a character in a short story. Read the part of Dan's essay shown here.

> Mrs. Wang is a practical, strong, caring, independent, and unselfish woman. Her practical nature comes out early in the story. She learns that she has to give a Buddhist priest ten dollars to get her dead husband out of purgatory. (Purgatory was where the dead went to be cleansed of earthly sins.) After years of prayer, only his right hand remains in purgatory. Mrs. Wang thinks about it. For ten dollars, she can buy enough food to last all winter. "If it's only one hand, he can pull himself out," she says firmly.

Review It

1. What is the thesis statement of Dan's essay?

_____

2. What details does Dan use to support his thesis statement?

_____

What Have You Learned in Unit 1?

Think about what you have learned about writing an expository essay. Use these questions to help you remember what was covered in Unit 1. Don't worry about writing complete sentences. Just record you own thoughts, ideas, and reactions.

1. How would you describe an expository essay to a class of younger students?

   _____

   _____

2. What is the purpose of the introduction to an essay?

   _____

3. Why is the body of the essay important?

   _____

4. Why do you need a conclusion?

   _____

5. Why is it important to state your main idea or thesis in the introduction to your essay?

   _____

6. How can your purpose for writing help you choose the best kind of expository essay?

   _____

7. Why is it important to organize your essay?

   _____

8. How do details improve your essay?

   _____

9. What can you do to make the connections between ideas clear for readers in an expository essay?

   _____

10. What are some strategies you can use to conclude your essay?

   _____

   _____

▶ If you can, share what you have learned in a group. Meet with other students to discuss the different styles of expository essays. Work together to make a list of "Five Great Ways to Explain Ideas Clearly."

UNIT 2 Writing to Explain

Writing is like walking. You take one step at a time. Writing an expository essay may seem like more than you can handle when you first think about doing it. If you break it into steps, each step will seem easier.

What to Do

Follow three basic steps as you write to explain. In this chapter, you will learn the three basic steps.

- Planning Your Writing
- Developing Your Writing
- Completing Your Writing

How to Do It

Keep this outline in mind. It shows the smaller steps within the three large ones.

Plan your writing.
Choose a topic.
Narrow the topic.
Identify the audience.
Identify the purpose.
Gather the details you need.
Organize your information.

Develop your writing.
Draft the introduction.
Draft the body.
Draft the conclusion.

Complete your writing.
Revise your essay.
Proofread your essay.
Publish your essay.

Apply It

▶ Imagine yourself writing exposition. Begin by looking for examples of expository writing in the everyday world. You may already have examples in your notebook from your work on page 13. If not, look in magazines, newspapers, and books. Choose one, and imagine that you were writing it. Visualize yourself going through each step. If you can, discuss the steps with a partner or group.

CHAPTER 1 Planning Your Writing

Writing begins even before you start your first draft. It starts even before you begin to make notes. Writing begins as soon as you begin thinking about your topic. Many of your first ideas will appear in the final draft of your writing. Taking the time to think and plan at the start will make that final draft as good as it can be.

What to Do

Plan what you want to say. Plan how to say it. You will have a much better chance of explaining clearly if you do.

How to Do It

Follow this checklist. In this chapter, you will work through all the steps that are needed to plan an expository essay. They are listed in this checklist.

☐ Start by choosing a topic that is important to you. Your essay will be strongest if you collect a few ideas for topics, and then choose the best one. List topics in your notebook.

☐ Once you have chosen your topic, narrow it until it fits your assignment and the space and time available to you. Use a topic web.

☐ Think about the people who will read your finished essay. You must make sure that they understand what you are saying. Complete audience profile forms.

☐ Decide what your purpose for writing is. The basic purpose of an expository essay is to tell your audience what you know about a topic.

☐ Gather the details you need to make your explanation clear. To strengthen your essay, you must expand your ideas with detailed facts. Make a list of sources.

☐ Organize your essay so that your audience will understand it. Use a planning chart.

Apply It

▶ As you complete the lessons in this chapter, return to this page to check off each step. You will be able to see the progress you are making.

Lesson 1   Choosing a Topic

Have you ever summarized a TV show for a friend? Have you ever explained how to load software onto a computer? Have you ever compared and contrasted the playing styles of two athletes? If you have, then you will know how to choose a topic for your expository essay.

What to Do

When you choose a topic for your expository essay, pick one that you want to learn more about. Choose something that interests you.

The topic you choose may determine what kind of essay you write. There are many types of expository essays. They include summaries of stories and books, how-to explanations, comparison-contrasts, cause-and-effect essays, and research reports.

How to Do It

Imagine that your teacher has assigned a three- to four-paragraph essay comparing and contrasting two people, places, or ideas.

Here are two lists of topics. Draw lines between items in the two lists that you could compare and contrast. Look for two things, people, or ideas that are alike in some way. The first one has been done for you.

Pueblo peoples of Southwest	Malcolm X
tornado	skateboarding
funny poem about dating	Cherokee Nation
Martin Luther King, Jr.	clothing fads of the 1900s
snowboarding	story about teen relationships
1995 sports coupe	hurricane
clothes of the 1800s	Henry Ford's Model-T Car

Review It

1. Of all the pairs above, which one would you like to write about?

_____

2. What do you think you might learn by comparing the two items you listed in question 1?

_____

_____

_____

Lesson 2 Narrowing a Topic

After you choose a topic, you may have to narrow it. Think about your assignment. Will the topic fit in the space you have? Will you run out of things to say? Will you run out of space before you cover all the important points?

What to Do

Think about what you want to accomplish. Suppose you decide to write an essay comparing all sports. You will need too much information to cover it. The topic is too large, too broad. You will have to narrow the topic.

How to Do It

A topic web can help you explore and then narrow your topic. Look at Darryl's topic web. He started out thinking that he would compare the sports of in-line skating and bicycling. That topic was too broad. There were too many points to discuss. He narrowed the topic down. He decided to compare safety issues for in-line skating and bicycling.

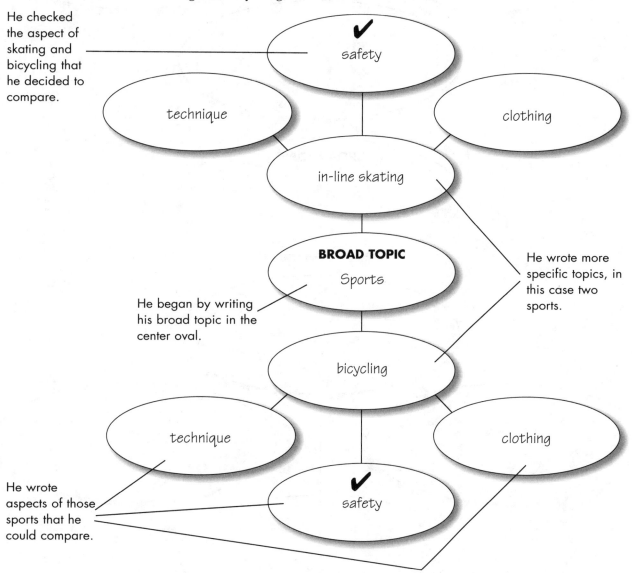

He checked the aspect of skating and bicycling that he decided to compare.

He began by writing his broad topic in the center oval.

He wrote more specific topics, in this case two sports.

He wrote aspects of those sports that he could compare.

Review It

▶ What other topics might Darryl have listed on his topic web? Add at least two topics to the web.

Apply It

▶ Use this web to narrow your topic. When you are finished, check the topic you will write about. If you are going to compare topics, check the two topics that you will compare.

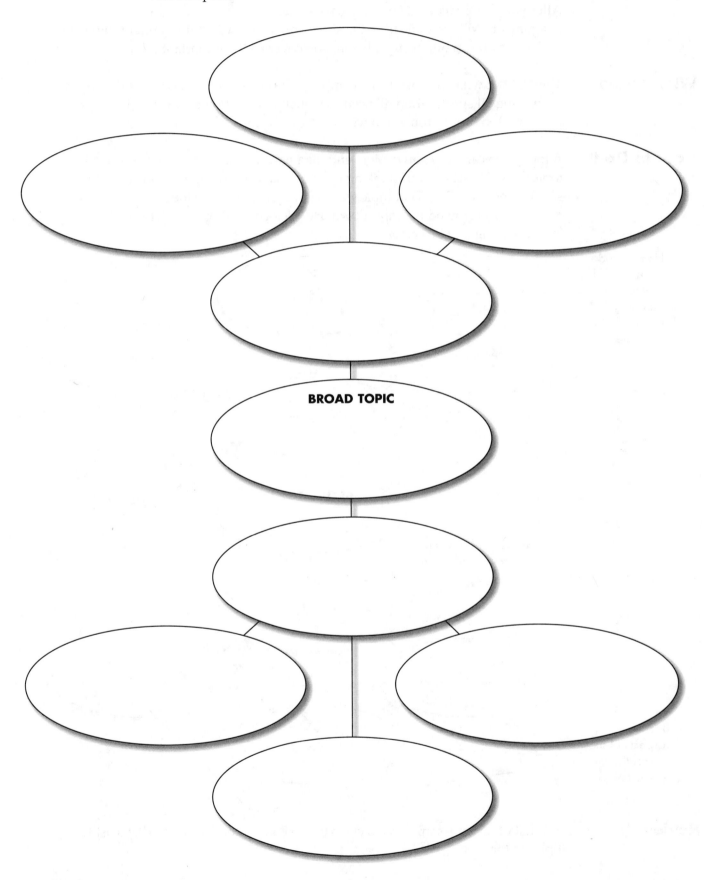

BROAD TOPIC

Lesson 3   Identifying the Audience

Your audience is the person or people who will read your essay. It is important to think about the interests and experiences of your audience when you write.

What to Do   Decide what your audience will know about your topic. What will they want to learn? Decide these things about your audience before you start to write. When you know your audience, you will know what kinds of details to include in your essay.

How to Do It   Darryl used an audience profile to identify and describe the people who would read his essay. This helped him know what kinds of details to use in his essay.

NARROWED TOPIC: Safety issues and equipment for in-line skating and bicycling	
AUDIENCE: high school students	
AGE RANGE: 14–18	
KNOWLEDGE REGARDING TOPIC: know basic safety rules of both sports know basic equipment needed	
OTHER FACTS THEY MAY NEED TO KNOW: which sport is safer what to look for in safety gear	
INTERESTS REGARDING TOPIC: may be concerned about which sport is more expensive to take up	

Review It   ▶ Read the following passage and decide what audience the writer had in mind.

Hey, you guys, zipping around on skates or bikes, listen up! Now you can be safe and look cool at the same time. Top sporting goods companies are making safety gear that is bright, bold, and beautiful. Why wear a plain black or white helmet when you can streak by in neon green?

1. Describe the audience that you think the writer had in mind.

_____

2. Underline the details that helped you identify the audience.

_____

Apply It   ▶ On a separate piece of paper, make a chart like Darryl's to identify your audience.

Lesson 4 Identifying the Purpose

The purpose of an essay is the reason it is written. The purpose of an expository essay is to explain.

What to Do

Think about the purpose of your essay. Decide what you want to do. Remember that different types of expository essays explain different things. Following are purposes for expository essays:

- Summarize a book or article.
- Compare two people, places, things, or ideas.
- Explain how to do something.
- Explain why something happens.

How to Do It

Let your purpose guide your writing. Here is a portion of Darryl's essay. He lets us know that his purpose is to compare and contrast kinds of athletes.

> There are sensible athletes, and there are "scarecrow" athletes. Remember the scarecrow in The Wizard of Oz? He didn't have a brain. He would be the kind of athlete you might see pedaling or skating down the yellow brick road without a helmet. The sensible athlete knows better.

Review It

▶ Here is another passage on the same topic. Decide what the purpose is.

> Both in-line skating and bicycling can be great fun, but both can also be dangerous. Modern safety equipment can make them fun and safe. For both sports, the first and most important piece of equipment is a helmet.

1. Underline the purpose in *What to Do* that best fits this passage.
2. Underline details in the passage that helped you identify the purpose.

Apply It

▶ What will be your purpose for writing your essay? Write one sentence stating your purpose.

_____

_____

Lesson 5   Gathering Information

If you know your purpose and your audience, you can decide what information to use in your essay. How will you find that information? Where will you look for it?

What to Do

Use reliable sources of information. The library is a great place to gather information. There you can find encyclopedias, magazines, newspapers, and books on your topic. Experts may be willing to give you information.

How to Do It

First, write the questions you want answered. Then make a list of sources that you can use to find the answers.

Before Darryl started his research, he wrote his questions on note cards. As he did his research, he used the cards to take notes.

What gear is needed for safe bicycling?

What gear is needed for safe in-line skating?

What are the biggest safety issues for bicycling?

What are the biggest safety issues for in-line skating?

Here is a list of sources Darryl planned to use to research his topic.

Library
   encyclopedia articles on bicycling and in-line skating
   books on these two sports
   bicycling and skating magazines
Ask Experts
   on-line bulletin board services
   Todd's brother—works for in-line skating company
   Pablo's father—used to race bicycles
Other Sources
   Visit sporting equipment stores; talk to sales people
   about latest equipment, prices, quality.

Apply It

▶ Write questions that you want your research to answer about your topic. Keep your purpose and audience in mind. Make a list of sources you might use to research your topic. Then research your topic.

Lesson 6 Organizing Information

After you have gathered the information for your essay, you need to organize it. Clear, logical organization helps your audience understand your ideas.

What to Do   Choose a method of organization that suits your topic and purpose.

How to Do It   Choose a method of organization and a graphic organizer from this chart.

PURPOSE	METHOD OF ORGANIZATION	GRAPHIC ORGANIZER
Summarize a story.	chronological order	plot map
Summarize a nonfiction work.	main ideas and details	outline
Compare two people, places, things, or ideas.	comparison and contrast	Venn diagram
Explain how to do something.	chronological order	chain of events
Explain why something happens.	cause and effect	numbered list 3 magma rises up through a crack 4 makes a channel and vent 1 pressure builds in magma chamber 2 forces the magma upward 5 gas and magma rush through channel out vent

Review It   ▶ After Darryl answered the questions on his note cards, he decided to use a Venn diagram to organize them. Here are two of Darryl's note cards. Add the notes from these two note cards to the Venn diagram below.

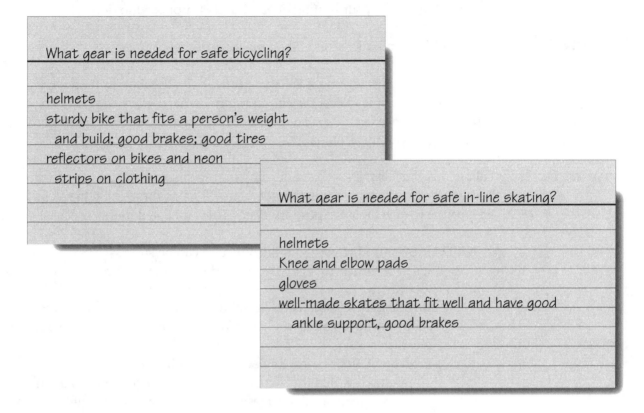

What gear is needed for safe bicycling?

helmets
sturdy bike that fits a person's weight
   and build; good brakes; good tires
reflectors on bikes and neon
   strips on clothing

What gear is needed for safe in-line skating?

helmets
Knee and elbow pads
gloves
well-made skates that fit well and have good
   ankle support, good brakes

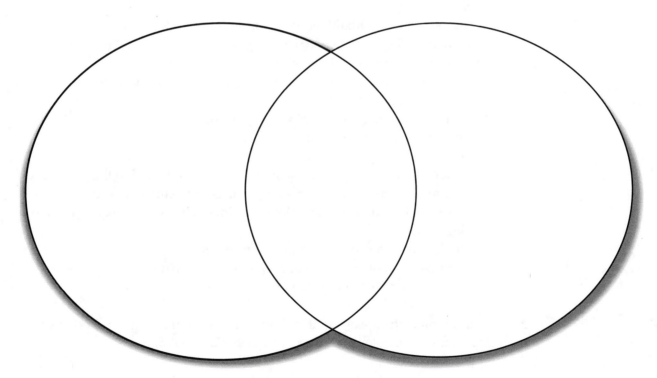

Apply It   ▶ Organize your notes. Create one of the graphic organizers shown on page 26. Put your notes into it.

CHAPTER 2 Developing Your Writing

As you write your drafts, work from your plan. Keep your audience and purpose in mind. Make sure your writing does what it is supposed to do.

What to Do

Get your ideas on paper. This is the time to write freely.

Each version of your writing is called a draft. To get the first draft on paper, start writing wherever it is easiest for you to begin. Perhaps you will want to begin by copying a sentence from your notes. Do not worry about spelling or grammar now. Just get your ideas on paper.

How to Do It

Follow this checklist. Develop your essay in three basic parts: an introduction, a body, and a conclusion. In this chapter, you will work through all the steps that are needed to develop an expository essay. They are listed in this checklist.

- ☐ Draft the introduction. Your introduction can be short.
  - ☐ Start your essay by letting your readers know what you are going to say. Identify the topic.
  - ☐ Include a thesis statement. Recall from Unit 1 that a thesis is a main idea about the information you have found. Follow these steps to develop a thesis statement:
    - ☐ Read all your notes. Review your graphic organizer.
    - ☐ Jot down words that sum up the most important information.
    - ☐ Write a sentence that states the main idea about this information.

- ☐ Draft the body. You identified your topic and included your thesis statement in the introduction. Now support that thesis statement in the body of your essay. Use facts, reasons and examples.
  - ☐ Use your notes to make sure that you use all of the facts you need to support your thesis statement.
  - ☐ Follow your graphic organizer to make sure that you present information in a clear order.

- ☐ Draft the conclusion. Your conclusion should be brief and to the point. You have already stated your main idea in a thesis statement and supported it with strong facts and reasons. Now it is time to bring your explanation to a strong close.
  - ☐ Include a sentence that restates your thesis.
  - ☐ End with a sentence that your readers will remember. It might be a quotation, a fact, or an anecdote.

Apply It

▶ As you complete the lessons in this chapter, return to this page to check off each step. You will be able to see the progress you are making.

Lesson 1   Drafting the Introduction

The introduction of your essay is where you tell readers what the essay is about. This is the place to grab their attention and make them want to keep reading.

What to Do   Consider these hints when you write your introduction.

- Use your notes. This way you will have your ideas and your facts in front of you when you write.
- Let your reader know right away what you are going to say.
- Begin with a question, a story, a funny quotation, or a startling fact to get your readers' attention.
- Include a thesis statement that expresses your main point.
- Remember that this is a draft. You can always go back and revise your introduction after you have completed the body of your essay.

How to Do It   Look at this example. It is the introduction of Darryl's essay. He lets readers know right away that he is going to compare safety issues for bicycling and in-line skating. In his thesis statement, he says that he thinks in-line skating is safer. He will build the rest of his essay around this idea.

> Is in-line skating safer than bicycling? Both bicycling and in-line skating are individual sports that offer plenty of exercise and fun. However, there are some safety issues about both sports to keep in mind. There has been a lot of publicity about injuries from in-line skating. Even so, in-line skating seems to be the safer of the two sports.

Apply It   ▶ Look over your notes. Form a thesis statement for your essay. Your thesis statement should express the main point you want to make about your topic.

▶ On a separate piece of paper, write your thesis statement.

▶ Now write the introduction to your essay. Write a first sentence that will grab your readers' attention and draw them in. Remember to include your thesis statement in your introduction.

Lesson 2 Drafting the Body

In your introduction, you have included your thesis statement. The body of your essay is where you will support this thesis statement with details.

What to Do   Consider these hints when you write the body of your essay.

- Organize your material. Then follow your organization as you write. This will make your writing easier and clearer.
- Use details, facts, and examples to develop your ideas and support your thesis statement.
- To keep ideas flowing between sentences and paragraphs, use transitional words and phrases. Transitions also signal readers that you are about to make a new point.

SOME TRANSITIONAL WORDS AND PHRASES

CHRONOLOGICAL ORDER	MAIN IDEAS AND DETAILS	COMPARISON AND CONTRAST	CAUSE AND EFFECT
first	more important	just as	because
next	most important	unlike	so
then	most of all	similarly	as a result
later	for example	both	for that reason
at the same time	such as	neither	if . . . then
meanwhile	that is	in contrast	therefore
before	like	different from	due to
after	in other words	similar to	thus
when	along with	like	consequently
soon	as follows	same as	since
as soon as	in this way	on the other hand	cause
finally	for instance	in the same way	make
after a while	as	equal to	create
in the end	namely	equally	determine

- Add factual support, statistics, or a quotation from an expert.
- In an essay that compares and contrasts two items, you can present information in either of two ways. You can tell all about one item in the first paragraph and all about the other item in the next paragraph, or you can discuss each item feature by feature.

How to Do It   Look at this example. Before Darryl wrote the body of his essay, he looked over his notes. He put check marks next to details that supported his thesis that in-line skating is the safer sport.

> What are habits of friends who ride bikes and skate?
>
> bicycling
>
>   tend not to wear helmets
>
>   usually ride on roads in traffic
>
>   follow most road rules
>
> in-line skating
>
> ✔ almost always wear helmets
>
> ✔ usually skate on paths, at indoor rinks, or in parks
>
> ✔ some have taken lessons that include safety tips

Darryl chose to compare his two items feature by feature. Here is a paragraph about helmets from Darryl's essay. Notice his use of transitional words and phrases.

> Both bicycle riders and in-line skaters should wear helmets. Studies show that helmets can reduce the risk of head injuries, especially to bicycle riders, by more than 60%. Most in-line skaters do wear helmets because helmets were part of the sport when it first became popular. On the other hand, many bicycle riders who did not wear helmets as young children tend not to wear them now.

Review It   ▶ Underline the transitional words and phrases in Darryl's paragraph.

Apply It   **1.** Write a list of the information that you will use to support your thesis statement.

_____

_____

_____

2. Check transitional words and phrases in the chart on page 30 that you can use to introduce the information you listed.

3. Now write the body of your essay on a separate sheet of paper. Use the transitional words and phrases from your list.

Lesson 3 Drafting the Conclusion

Use the conclusion to sum up the points that you have made in your essay. Reinforce the main point, or thesis statement, that you made in your introduction. Show how you formed your ideas.

What to Do

Consider these hints when you write the conclusion of your essay.

- Summarize your information.
- Remind your readers how your thesis statement is supported. Point out that you provided one or more of the following kinds of support:
  - Reasons.
  - Examples.
  - Expert opinions.
  - Comparisons.
- Use your conclusion to make the strongest point in the body stand out. Make a final comment on that point or give an example to support it.
- Restate your thesis or refer to your introduction.

How to Do It

Here is Darryl's conclusion. Notice that he summarizes the comparison and clearly restates his thesis.

> As individual sports, bicycling and in-line skating both offer plenty of exercise and fun. Wearing the proper gear and following the rules of these two sports should provide safety. However, as my comparison showed, more skaters than bicycle riders use safety equipment. Therefore, after reading and talking with friends and experts, I think that in-line skating is the safer choice

Review It

▶ What is the main point, or thesis, of Darryl's essay?

_____

_____

Apply It

▶ Now write your conclusion on a separate piece of paper.

CHAPTER 3 Completing Your Writing

After the first draft is written, return to it to make it better. Revise it to make it stronger. Proofread it to make it correct. Then publish it to bring it to your audience.

What to Do

Make your writing better with every draft. Revise the first draft to make a second draft that is better. Keep working at your drafts until your essay says just what you want it to say as well as you can say it. Draft, revise, and revise again until you are pleased with your work.

How to Do It

Follow this checklist. In this chapter, you will work through all the steps that are needed to complete an expository essay. They are listed in this checklist.

☐ Revise your essay. Now that you have your ideas down on paper, it is time to go back and revise. When you revise, you make changes to make sure that you have expressed your ideas clearly.
☐ Read your draft carefully.
☐ Use the revision checklist on page 35 to correct and strengthen your writing.

☐ Proofread your essay. Fix any mistakes in spelling, grammar, and punctuation.
☐ Read your revised draft sentence by sentence and word by word. Look for the little mistakes that you might have missed or ignored earlier.
☐ Use the proofreading checklist on page 36 to find and correct any mistakes.

☐ Publish your essay to bring it to your audience.
☐ Choose a way of publishing that will bring your ideas to your audience's attention.
☐ Follow the requirements of the method you choose.

Apply It

▶ As you complete the lessons in this chapter, return to this page to check off each step. You will be able to see the progress you are making.

Lesson 1   Revising Your Essay

Now that you have a draft of your essay, go back and revise. Make changes that will improve your work.

What to Do   Make improvements in your work.

Start by reading what you have written. Don't make changes now. Just read.

Now read it again. This time, begin making changes. Use the revision checklist on the next page to guide your work. Keep making changes until your writing says just what you want it to say. Above all, make sure that you have expressed your ideas clearly.

How to Do It   Here is part of Darryl's revised essay. Notice how he applied the items in the revision checklist.

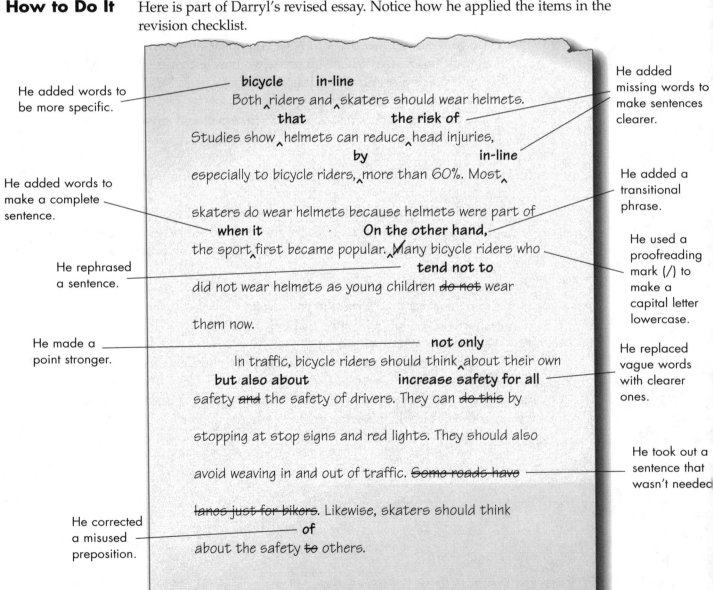

He added words to be more specific.

He added words to make a complete sentence.

He rephrased a sentence.

He made a point stronger.

He corrected a misused preposition.

He added missing words to make sentences clearer.

He added a transitional phrase.

He used a proofreading mark (/) to make a capital letter lowercase.

He replaced vague words with clearer ones.

He took out a sentence that wasn't needed.

bicycle   in-line
Both ˄riders and ˄skaters should wear helmets.
          that   the risk of
Studies show ˄helmets can reduce ˄head injuries,
                          by   in-line
especially to bicycle riders, ˄more than 60%. Most˄

skaters do wear helmets because helmets were part of
          when it   On the other hand,
the sport ˄first became popular. ˄Many bicycle riders who
                              tend not to
did not wear helmets as young children ~~do not~~ wear

them now.
                                          not only
In traffic, bicycle riders should think ˄about their own
          but also about   increase safety for all
safety ~~and~~ the safety of drivers. They can ~~do this~~ by

stopping at stop signs and red lights. They should also

avoid weaving in and out of traffic. ~~Some roads have~~

~~lanes just for bikers.~~ Likewise, skaters should think
                        of
about the safety ~~to~~ others.

Apply It

▶ Use this revision checklist to guide you as you revise your work.

INTRODUCTION

☐ Use your introduction to get your readers' attention. If it does not, open your essay with a funny or interesting story, a shocking or startling fact, an interesting quotation, or a question that makes readers think.

☐ Include a thesis statement that expresses your main point. If you have not, review your notes. Form an opinion about your topic. Use this as the basis for your thesis statement.

BODY

☐ Focus on the main purpose, which is to explain. If you have not, identify the places where your essay gets away from the main purpose.

☐ Include only details that support your thesis statement. If you have details that do not, take them out. Add details that do.

☐ Follow a clear organizational plan throughout the essay. If you have not, reorder details.

☐ Use transitions to make ideas flow smoothly. If you have not, add transitional words and phrases.

☐ Explain your topic thoroughly. If you have not, check your notes. Find information that you can include to make your explanation more complete. Do more research, if necessary.

CONCLUSION

☐ Sum up the main points you made in your essay. Read over the introduction and body of your essay to recall the main points. Add them to your conclusion if you have not already done so.

☐ Reinforce your thesis statement and show how you formed it. If you have not, reread your introduction. Restate your thesis statement in different words. Add a phrase or a sentence that tells how you formed this idea.

▶ Sometimes it helps to have another person read your writing. Ask a classmate to read your essay. Pick a person who can point out the good parts of your essay and who can suggest ways to improve it.

Here is a list of questions your reader can use as a guide. What else would you like your reader to check? Add it to the bottom of the list.

- Can you tell what the purpose of my essay is?
- Have I achieved my purpose?
- Can you tell what audience I had in mind?
- Have I included the information that my audience needs to understand me?
- Are my ideas organized clearly? Do my ideas make sense?

Lesson 2 Proofreading Your Essay

No one wants to turn in a paper that has mistakes. You can avoid this by proofreading your essay.

What to Do

When you proofread, look for the little mistakes that you might have missed or ignored earlier.

When you are writing a draft, it is a good idea not to worry about grammar and spelling. When you are revising, you should focus on improving the meaning of your essay. Now it is time to look for those mistakes in grammar and spelling. Read your work sentence by sentence and word by word. Use the proofreading checklist below to find and correct any mistakes.

How to Do It

Use the following checklist. It lists problems you may find in expository writing. You also will find a guide to grammar, mechanics, and usage on pages 76–80.

☐ Make subjects agree with their verbs in number. (Singular subjects need singular verbs. Plural subjects need plural verbs.)
☐ Use complete sentences. Correct any fragments. Correct any run-on sentences.
☐ Use pronouns correctly. Is it clear what noun each pronoun refers to?
☐ Use adjectives to modify nouns or pronouns. Use adverbs to modify verbs, adjectives, and other adverbs.
☐ End each sentence with a period, question mark, or exclamation point.
☐ Use apostrophes correctly in all contractions, to show where letters have been taken out.
☐ Use apostrophes correctly to show possession.
☐ Check the essay for spelling errors. If you are unsure about the spelling of certain words, use a dictionary.

Here are some marks you can use when you proofread. Notice how Darryl used these marks.

^ Insert letters or words here.	**have** Most of you ^ probably been riding a two-wheeler since
Capitalize this ≡ letter.	**were** you ~~was~~ very young. on the other hand, many of you
/ Make this letter lowercase.	
— Delete or replace this.	may have never tried to stand up on I̶n-line skates.

Apply It

▶ Use the proofreading checklist to find errors in your work. After you proofread your essay, ask a classmate to proofread it. A new reader can often catch mistakes that you have missed.

Lesson 3 Publishing Your Essay

You can share your essay with readers by publishing it. There are many ways you can choose to do this.

What to Do   Find the best way to reach your audience.

How will you publish your essay? How can you be sure that your audience will see it or hear it? If you can, discuss ideas with a group of students. Consider everyone's suggestions, and then choose the plan that you feel is right.

How to Do It   Choose a way of publishing that suits your audience. Here are some ways other writers chose.

Audience	Ways to Publish
Students or adults at school	■ Send your expository essay to the school newspaper. ■ Read your essay to your class. ■ Make a poster to go with your essay. Include a pocket with copies for students to take.
Audiences outside school	■ Submit your expository essay to a magazine. ■ Post your expository essay on an on-line bulletin board. ■ Duplicate copies for family and friends.

Apply It

1. Think of two ways to publish your essay. Write your ideas here. Then put a check mark beside the idea you like better.

_____

_____

2. Make a clean copy of your essay. Publish your essay in the way you chose.

What Have You Learned in Unit 2?

Use these questions to gather and review your thoughts about each of the key points in Unit 2. Don't worry about writing complete sentences. Just put some thoughts, ideas, and reactions down for each question.

1. Write one good topic for a three-to-five-paragraph expository essay.

_____

2. Why is it a good topic?

_____

3. What kind of information do you need in an expository essay?

_____

4. What key statement should you put in the introduction to an expository essay?

_____

5. What should you do in the body of an expository essay?

_____

6. What should you put in the conclusion of an expository essay?

_____

7. What do you do when you revise?

_____

8. What do you do when you proofread?

_____

9. What did you learn about your topic as you wrote your expository essay?

_____

10. What can you do next time to make the writing easier and more enjoyable?

_____

▶ Meet with other students. Share what you have learned in a group. Brainstorm a list of guidelines for writing expository essays. Then make a poster listing these guidelines. Try to come up with a catchy title for your poster. Hang your poster where other students can use it for their own writing.

UNIT 3 Writing on Your Own

There are many types of expository writing. You are already familiar with essays that compare and contrast, solve a problem, or explore cause and effect. These different types of essays have the same purpose. They are written to explain and inform.

What to Do   Become familiar with the three different kinds of expository essays that you will write in this unit.

> A Summary of a Story
> A How-to Essay
> A Comparison-and-Contrast Essay

How to Do It   Learn the key elements of each kind of essay that you will write.

A summary of a story tells what the story is about. A summary takes much less space than the original story. It has far fewer words. The summary gives some background information about the story and focuses on the high points. You summarize a story when you write a book report.

A how-to explanation tells readers how to do something. A recipe is a how-to explanation. So are the instructions that come with games, models, or electronic equipment. When you write a how-to explanation, explain something that you can do well. You will be teaching your readers how to do it, too.

A comparison-and-contrast essay shows how subjects are alike and different. It may show an interesting difference between two subjects that are alike. Or, it may show an interesting likeness between two subjects that are different. The writer states a thesis about how the two subjects are related.

Review It   ▶ Find examples of each type of expository writing that you will write in this unit.

▶ Look for summaries in magazines and textbooks. You can also find books of summaries in the reference section of a library. Look for how-to explanations in magazines and newspapers. Magazines about crafts and hobbies are especially good sources. Look for comparison-and-contrast articles in consumer magazines. You can also find them in magazines about particular interests. For example, a magazine about computers may compare two brands. Save the examples in your notebook.

CHAPTER 1 Summarizing a Story

Have you ever read a book that you wanted to share with a friend? You can write a summary to tell, briefly, what it is about.

What to Do

Learn what is unique about a summary. In a summary, you share what you know about a book. You tell enough so that others can decide whether they want to read the book.

How to Do It

Look at this example. It is a summary that a student named Asia wrote.

INTRODUCTION
She named the book and author, stated the setting, and named the major characters.

> Roll of Thunder, Hear My Cry is a novel by Mildred C. Taylor. It tells about the Logans, an African-American family in Mississippi during the Great Depression.

BODY
She described the conflict at the start of the book.

She told the most important events in order.

> The Logans are poor. Mr. Logan has to leave home to work for the railroad. Mrs. Logan is a teacher. Their daughter, Cassie, is forced to go to a segregated school. However, the Logans own their farm land and are happy as a family.
>
> Trouble comes to the Logans when they mortgage their land to help sharecroppers buy food. A plantation owner and his men begin to bother them. There are night raids, and shots are fired. Mrs. Logan loses her job. Then Mr. Logan breaks his leg in an accident. The plantation owner threatens to take the Logans' land away.

CONCLUSION
She told what happens at the end of the story.

> In the end, the whole family fights against the night raiders. Help comes when Cassie's uncle brings them money to pay their mortgage. The farm is saved!

Review It

1. What is the title of the book that Asia summarized?

_____

2. List two important events that Asia mentioned in the summary.

_____

_____

3. How did the story conclude?

_____

Lesson 1   Mapping a Story

Look in the library or at your own books. Which books do you remember reading? Which ones made you laugh or made you cry? Did any of the characters remind you of yourself or someone else? Choose a favorite book to summarize. It will be more fun to summarize a book that you enjoyed reading.

What to Do

Focus on important details. The details you include in your summary will tell your readers what the book is about. A summary should be short, so you cannot include every detail. The key to writing a good summary is deciding what details are important.

How to Do It

A story map can help you recognize important details. Here is the story map that Asia created for her summary of *Roll of Thunder, Hear My Cry.*

STORY MAP

Title:	Roll of Thunder, Hear My Cry	
Setting:	the Logan family farm in Mississippi, Depression era	
Characters:	Mr. Logan	plantation owner
	Mrs. Logan	plantation owner's helpers
	Cassie Logan	Cassie's uncle
Conflict (Problem):	Logans help sharecroppers, which angers plantation owner.	
Event:	Logans mortgage their land to help sharecroppers buy food.	
Event:	Plantation owner starts trouble.	
Event:	Night raids.	
Event:	Mrs. Logan loses her job.	
Event:	Mr. Logan breaks his leg.	
Event:	Plantation owner threatens to take the land away.	
Event:	The night raiders are fought off.	
Event:	Help comes from an uncle.	
Solution:	The mortgage is paid, and the farm is saved.	

Apply It ▶ Use this story map to take notes for your summary. Follow the order of your book. List the characters, events, and details that seem important.

▶ Study your story map. Put check marks beside the characters, events, and details that are *most* important to the story. Cross out details that are less important.

STORY MAP

Title:		
Setting:		
Characters:		
Conflict (Problem):		
Event:		
Event:		
Event:		
Event:		
Event:		
Event:		
Event:		
Event:		
Event:		
Event:		
Solution:		

Lesson 2   Drafting Your Summary

Draft the three main parts of your summary: the introduction, the body, and the conclusion.

What to Do   Consider these hints when you write your summary.

- Plan to keep the introduction to two or three sentences. First, identify the book. Give its title and author. Then describe the setting and name the major characters.
- If you can, keep the body to no more than three paragraphs. *Briefly* tell what the conflict or problem is at the start of the book. Then describe the important events that lead to the climax, or the high point. Remember that you are not writing the book. The author has already done that. Tell *your* readers what the story is about as clearly and as briefly as you can.
- Plan to keep your conclusion to two or three sentences. You can tell the end of the story, the main idea of the book, or what you think the author's message was.

How to Do It   Use a drafting chart. Write the notes from your story map as complete sentences. Here is the drafting chart that Asia used for her summary.

INTRODUCTION
She named the book and author, stated the setting, and named the major characters.

> <u>Roll of Thunder, Hear My Cry</u> was written by Mildred C.
>   Taylor.
> It is a novel.
> It takes place in Mississippi during the Great Depression.
> People were very poor during this time.
> The book is about the Logan family.
> Mr. and Mrs. Logan both work.
> Cassie has to go to a segregated school.

BODY
She described the conflict at the start of the book.
She told the most important events in order.

> The Logans mortgage their land to help sharecroppers
>   buy food.
> The plantation owner wants their land, so he and his two
>   mean helpers start trouble.
> There are night raids on the Logans' farm.
> Mrs. Logan loses her job.
> Mr. Logan gets injured.
> The plantation owner threatens to take their land away.

CONCLUSION
She told what happens at the end of the story.

> The family fights back against the night raiders.
> An uncle comes to help with the mortgage.
> The mortgage is paid.
> The farm is saved.

Apply It

▶ Use this drafting chart to draft the three basic parts of your summary. Use your notes from the story map on page 42. Write your notes as complete sentences. Remember that this is just your first draft. You do not have to worry about grammar and spelling now. Get your ideas on paper. You will revise your work later.

INTRODUCTION
Give the book and the author. State the setting and name the major characters.

BODY
Tell the most important events in order.

CONCLUSION
Keep your conclusion short. Tell the end of the story.

Lesson 3 Completing Your Summary

Revise your draft to improve it. Remember that it should be brief but complete enough so that a reader can tell what happens in the book.

What to Do

After you have written your draft, read it. Then revise it. When you have revised your draft, proofread it to find any mistakes in spelling, capitalization, punctuation, and grammar.

How to Do It

Use the revision checklist on page 35 and the one on page 46, which focuses on key elements of a summary. Use the proofreading checklist on page 36 and the one on page 46, which lists problems to be especially careful about in a summary.

Look at this example. It is part of Asia's first draft. She used the revision and proofreading checklists to make improvements and fix mistakes.

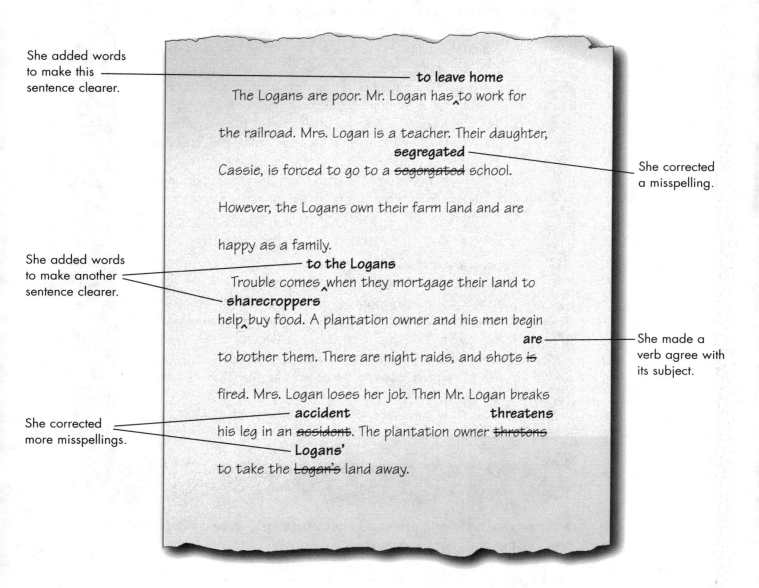

She added words to make this sentence clearer.

to leave home

The Logans are poor. Mr. Logan has ^to work for

the railroad. Mrs. Logan is a teacher. Their daughter,

segregated

Cassie, is forced to go to a ~~segergated~~ school.

She corrected a misspelling.

However, the Logans own their farm land and are

happy as a family.

She added words to make another sentence clearer.

to the Logans

Trouble comes ^when they mortgage their land to

sharecroppers

help ^buy food. A plantation owner and his men begin

are

to bother them. There are night raids, and shots ~~is~~

She made a verb agree with its subject.

fired. Mrs. Logan loses her job. Then Mr. Logan breaks

accident   **threatens**

his leg in an ~~accident~~. The plantation owner ~~throtens~~

She corrected more misspellings.

Logans'

to take the ~~Logan's~~ land away.

Apply It

▶ After you have written the draft, read it. Then revise it. Use the checklist on page 35 and the one below, which focuses on key elements of a summary.

▶ When you have revised your draft, proofread it. Fix any mistakes in spelling, capitalization, punctuation, and grammar. Use the checklist on page 36 and the one below, which lists problems to be especially careful about in a summary.

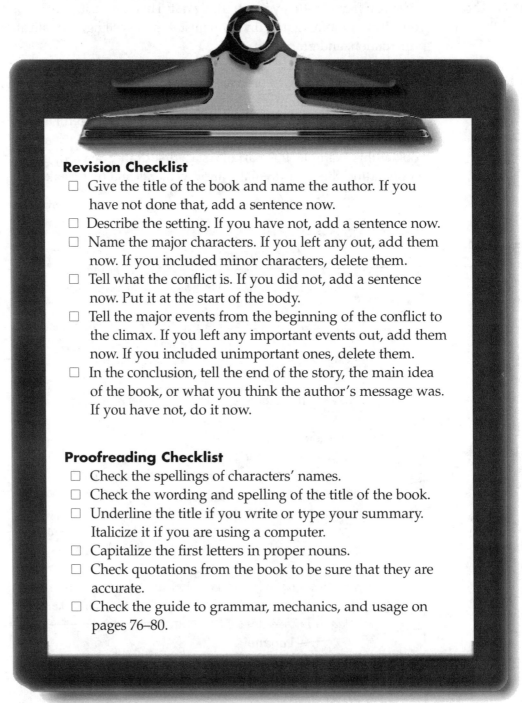

Revision Checklist
☐ Give the title of the book and name the author. If you have not done that, add a sentence now.
☐ Describe the setting. If you have not, add a sentence now.
☐ Name the major characters. If you left any out, add them now. If you included minor characters, delete them.
☐ Tell what the conflict is. If you did not, add a sentence now. Put it at the start of the body.
☐ Tell the major events from the beginning of the conflict to the climax. If you left any important events out, add them now. If you included unimportant ones, delete them.
☐ In the conclusion, tell the end of the story, the main idea of the book, or what you think the author's message was. If you have not, do it now.

Proofreading Checklist
☐ Check the spellings of characters' names.
☐ Check the wording and spelling of the title of the book.
☐ Underline the title if you write or type your summary. Italicize it if you are using a computer.
☐ Capitalize the first letters in proper nouns.
☐ Check quotations from the book to be sure that they are accurate.
☐ Check the guide to grammar, mechanics, and usage on pages 76–80.

▶ If you can, revise and proofread with a partner. Use the checklists to think of ways to improve your summaries.

▶ Make a clean copy of your summary. You may want to put it into a folder. On the cover, you could illustrate one of the important events in the book.

CHAPTER 2 Writing a How-to Explanation

A how-to explanation does just what its name says. It tells readers how to do something. A how-to explanation may tell how to make stew. It may explain how to assemble a table that comes in pieces. It may give directions on how to live a happy life.

What to Do

Explain something that you can do well. By following your directions, readers should be able to do it, too.

How to Do It

Look at this example. It is Julio's how-to explanation for making pita-bread pizzas.

INTRODUCTION
He told what he would explain.

BODY
He told what would be needed to do the job.

He told what to do, step by step.

CONCLUSION
He gave extra information that might be useful.

> Wouldn't a slice of pizza taste great right now? Making pita-bread pizzas is easy and fun. This is the way I do it for my friends. This recipe will serve four.
>
> Before you begin cooking, gather the following ingredients: two pita pockets, one eight-ounce jar of tomato sauce, six ounces of mozzarella cheese, and oregano, garlic, and red pepper flakes. You will also need a cheese grater and a broiling pan.
>
> Shred the cheese by using a cheese grater or by cutting it up into very small pieces. Split each pita pocket in half by cutting it around the rim. Then you will have four round pizza crusts. Spread four tablespoons of sauce on each crust. Sprinkle equal amounts of cheese on top of each pizza. Add oregano, garlic, and red pepper flakes to taste.
>
> Place the pizzas on a broiling pan. Turn the oven to "broil" and put the pan on the broiling rack. Broil until the cheese starts to brown on the top. This should take five to seven minutes.
>
> Serve the pizza piping hot! People can add more seasonings if they like. Adjust the amounts for different numbers of people. Have fun!

Review It

1. According to Julio, what should you do just before you split the pita in half?

_____

2. According to Julio, what should you do right after you split the pita in half?

_____

3. Underline a sentence that states something that you do not have to do but might want to do.

Lesson 1   Deciding What the Audience Needs

People read how-to explanations to learn how to do something. For some of them, the topic may be completely new. Others may know something about the topic, but need to know more. Figure out what your readers already know. Then figure out what they need to know.

What to Do   Make your how-to explanation clear *for your audience*. To do that, you have to think about them. What is their background? What do they know? What do they need to know?

How to Do It   Make an audience profile. Before Julio wrote his essay, he created an audience profile. He figured out what his audience knew. Then he figured out what they would need to know.

WHO IS YOUR AUDIENCE? friends, younger brothers and sisters

WHAT WILL THEY KNOW ABOUT THIS TOPIC? some ingredients that are usually in pizza, how many people they expect to feed, what pita bread is

---

WHAT WILL THEY NEED TO KNOW? other ingredients and cooking tools; definitions of terms (shred, broil, slice); how much of each ingredient they will need

---

WHY DO THEY WANT TO KNOW THIS? so that they don't buy too little or too much, so that they know how many they will make

---

WHAT SHOULD YOU KEEP IN MIND ABOUT YOUR AUDIENCE? they do not like to make anything too complicated

---

Review It   **1.** For what people did Julio decide to write his explanation?

_____

2. List one thing that Julio would *not* have to explain for his audience.

_____

3. List two things that Julio *would* have to explain for his audience.

_____

_____

Apply It

▶ Think of two possible audiences for your how-to explanation. Use the following forms to make a profile for each one. Choose one as your final audience.

WHO IS YOUR AUDIENCE?
WHAT WILL THEY KNOW ABOUT THIS TOPIC?
WHAT WILL THEY NEED TO KNOW?
WHY DO THEY WANT TO KNOW THIS?
WHAT SHOULD YOU KEEP IN MIND ABOUT YOUR AUDIENCE?

WHO IS YOUR AUDIENCE?
WHAT WILL THEY KNOW ABOUT THIS TOPIC?
WHAT WILL THEY NEED TO KNOW?
WHY DO THEY WANT TO KNOW THIS?
WHAT SHOULD YOU KEEP IN MIND ABOUT YOUR AUDIENCE?

▶ When you have finished your profiles, work with a partner if you can. Talk about the audiences you have profiled. Decide which one you would most like to reach. Choose that one audience for your how-to explanation.

Lesson 2 Organizing by Sequence

What happens if you follow directions out of order? What if you skip a step? If you were building a house, you might find that there is no staircase to climb to the second floor. If you were making a pizza, you could end up eating toasted crust with no topping.

What to Do

Remember to arrange the steps in order. It is also important not to leave any steps out.

How to Do It

Use a step chain. It helps you to list steps in a process and then re-order them in the right sequence.

Julio used a step chain to organize his explanation for making pizza. First, he listed the steps in the boxes on the left. He tried to follow the steps in his mind. When he did this, he saw some mistakes. Julio then revised the list in the boxes on the right. Here is the step chain he made.

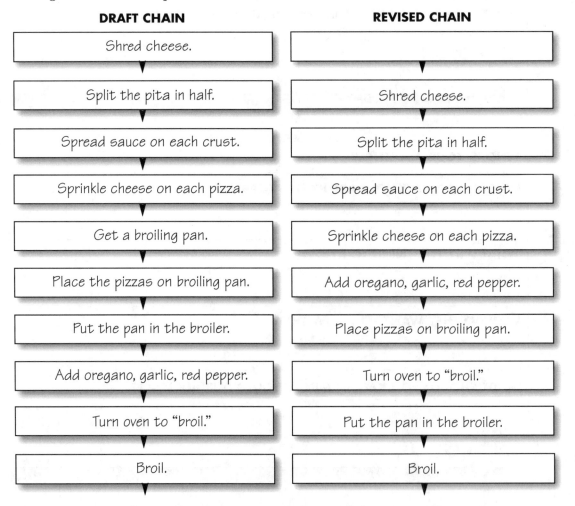

DRAFT CHAIN

- Shred cheese.
- Split the pita in half.
- Spread sauce on each crust.
- Sprinkle cheese on each pizza.
- Get a broiling pan.
- Place the pizzas on broiling pan.
- Put the pan in the broiler.
- Add oregano, garlic, red pepper.
- Turn oven to "broil."
- Broil.

REVISED CHAIN

- Shred cheese.
- Split the pita in half.
- Spread sauce on each crust.
- Sprinkle cheese on each pizza.
- Add oregano, garlic, red pepper.
- Place pizzas on broiling pan.
- Turn oven to "broil."
- Put the pan in the broiler.
- Broil.

▶ In the draft, Julio had the readers add oregano, garlic, and red pepper after placing the pizza in the broiler. He decided that this wasn't a good idea. Why?

Apply It   ▶ Use this step chain to list the steps in your explanation. First, list the steps in the draft chain on the left. Then look over the steps. Try to follow the steps in your mind. Are any steps out of order? Are any missing? If so, make a revised chain of steps on the right.

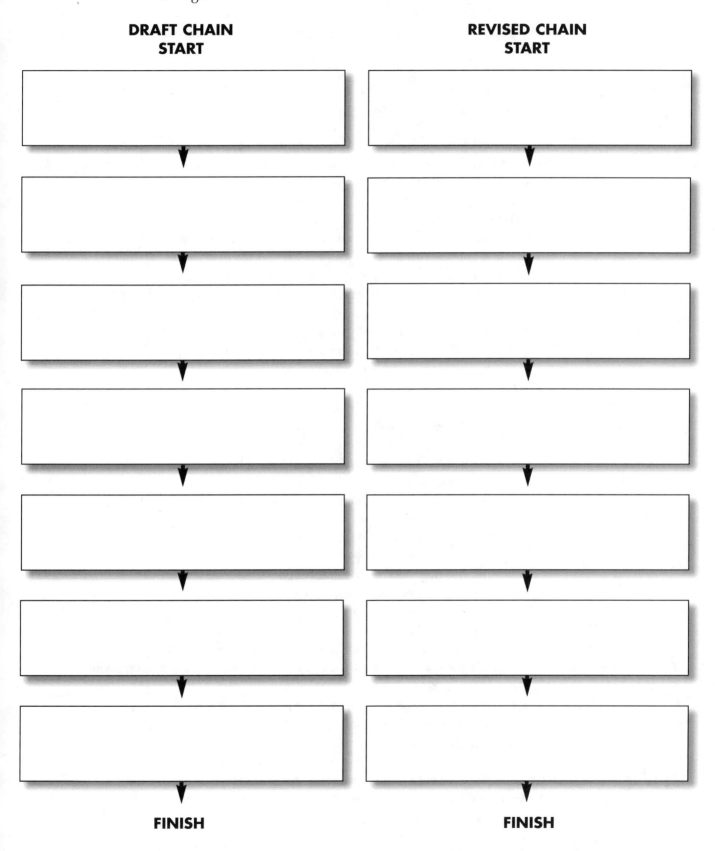

**DRAFT CHAIN
START**

**REVISED CHAIN
START**

FINISH

FINISH

Lesson 3 Drafting Your How-to Explanation

You have done your planning and completed your step chart. You know who your audience will be. Now it is time to draft your explanation. In the drafting stage, the point is to get your words on paper. Focus on what you want to say. You can improve the way you say it later.

What to Do

Give your explanation an introduction, take your readers through the process step-by-step, and then conclude.

How to Do It

You can begin at the beginning and work right through the draft. This is one way to write a draft. If it doesn't work for you, start somewhere else. Many writers like to start with the body. They write the introduction later.

Draft the Introduction
☐ Begin with a sentence that will grab your readers' interest.
- Think about the final result of the process (such as a tasty pizza).
- Think about why your audience will like the result.
- Write a sentence or question about that (such as "Wouldn't a slice of pizza taste great right now?"
☐ Tell your readers what you are going to teach them to do.
☐ Give them information they need in advance (such as how many people a recipe serves).

Draft the Body
☐ Tell readers what steps to follow.
☐ Look over your step chart. Use it to keep the steps in order.
☐ Look at your audience profile to decide what details your audience may need to know.
- They may need to have some steps explained (such as how to shred cheese).
- They may need to have terms defined or explained (such as *broil*).
- They may need to have more specific information (such as how much sauce to use).

Draft the Conclusion
☐ Add information that is interesting but not absolutely necessary.
- It may tell them how to adjust the directions (to serve more people, for example).
- It may suggest another way to get the job done.
☐ End with a sentence that will make your readers want to follow your directions.

Apply It

▶ On a separate sheet of paper, draft your how-to explanation. Use the notes and plans you have made as you write. Do not worry about spelling and grammar right now. Get your ideas down on paper.

Lesson 4 Completing Your How-to Explanation

Give your essay the final touches that will make it the best it can be. Remember a how-to explanation tells readers how to do something. Make sure that each step is clear and complete.

What to Do

After you have written the draft, read it. Then revise it. When you have revised your draft, proofread it. Fix any mistakes in spelling, capitalization, punctuation, and grammar.

How to Do It

Use the revision checklist on page 35 and the one below, which focuses on key elements of a how-to explanation. Use the proofreading checklist on page 36 and the one below, which lists problems to be careful about in a how-to explanation.

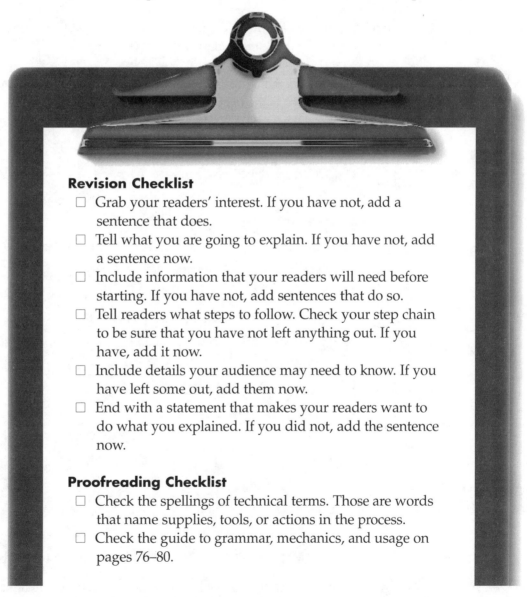

Revision Checklist
- ☐ Grab your readers' interest. If you have not, add a sentence that does.
- ☐ Tell what you are going to explain. If you have not, add a sentence now.
- ☐ Include information that your readers will need before starting. If you have not, add sentences that do so.
- ☐ Tell readers what steps to follow. Check your step chain to be sure that you have not left anything out. If you have, add it now.
- ☐ Include details your audience may need to know. If you have left some out, add them now.
- ☐ End with a statement that makes your readers want to do what you explained. If you did not, add the sentence now.

Proofreading Checklist
- ☐ Check the spellings of technical terms. Those are words that name supplies, tools, or actions in the process.
- ☐ Check the guide to grammar, mechanics, and usage on pages 76–80.

Apply It

▶ Make the changes that you think will improve your how-to explanation. You may want to use illustrations to make your how-to even clearer. Make a clean copy of your explanation. If a computer is available, use it to prepare your final copy.

CHAPTER 3 Comparing and Contrasting

In an essay that compares and contrasts, the writer looks at similarities and differences between two subjects. The subjects might be people, places, or things.

What to Do

Write about *two* subjects and how they are related. Here are some guidelines.

- Choose two subjects that are alike in some ways but different in other ways.
- Open with a thesis statement about how the two subjects are related.
- Gather details that support your thesis statement.
- Arrange the details and ideas in a clear order. Follow that order throughout the essay.
- Use transitions to make the comparison clear. Some examples are: *like, in the same way, both, unlike,* and *on the other hand.*

How to Do It

Look at this example. Jani chose to write an essay comparing and contrasting two favorite authors. Here is the beginning of Jani's essay.

INTRODUCTION
She told what she would compare. She stated a thesis.

Many readers enjoy books by both Shel Silverstein and Robert Cormier. Each of them writes from a unique point of view. However, both authors use strange situations and endings that readers do not expect.

BODY
She told about each writer in a separate paragraph. This is one way to organize a comparison and contrast.

Shel Silverstein has been honored by the American Library Association. His most famous book is Where the Sidewalk Ends. It is a collection of poetry for young readers. Most of his poems are funny, but they have twists in them. When you finish a poem, you are often surprised.

Robert Cormier is also an award-winning writer. His novel The Chocolate War was named Best Book for Young Adults by the American Library Association. Most of his novels are about people who are in trouble. They often have disturbing endings.

CONCLUSION
She returned to her thesis.

Both authors write about subjects that interest teenage readers. They take their readers into weird situations and make them think about a world without happy endings.

Review It

▶ Underline sentences that state ways that the two authors are alike.

Apply It

▶ Choose two subjects (people, places, or things) to compare and contrast. Write them in your notebook.

Lesson 1   Selecting Important Details

What to Do

Before you write your essay, you must gather information for it. You must decide what information is important.

List the features of each subject you are going to write about. Arrange them in a way that lets you see similarities and differences. Decide which features are most important.

Then think about the similarities and differences you have found. Sum them up in a statement. This will be your thesis statement.

How to Do It

Use a Venn diagram to compare features of the two subjects you have chosen.

Jani used a Venn diagram. In it, she listed facts about each author. She included what was different about them. Then she listed what was the same. When she was finished, she had a clear picture of how the two authors were alike and how they were different.

Then she thought about the similarities and differences and wrote the first draft of her thesis statement.

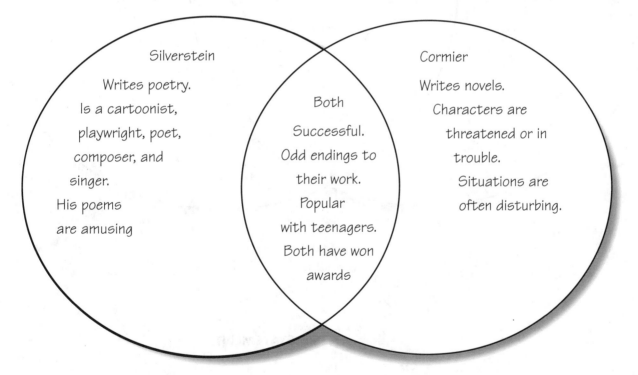

Silverstein

Writes poetry.
Is a cartoonist,
playwright, poet,
composer, and
singer.
His poems
are amusing

Both

Successful.
Odd endings to
their work.
Popular
with teenagers.
Both have won
awards

Cormier

Writes novels.
Characters are
threatened or in
trouble.
Situations are
often disturbing.

THESIS STATEMENT:

Both authors use strange situations and endings that readers do not expect.

Apply It

▶ Study the subjects that you will compare. Identify ways that they are similar and different. List these similarities and differences in the Venn diagram.

▶ Then think about the similarities and differences and write the first draft of your thesis statement.

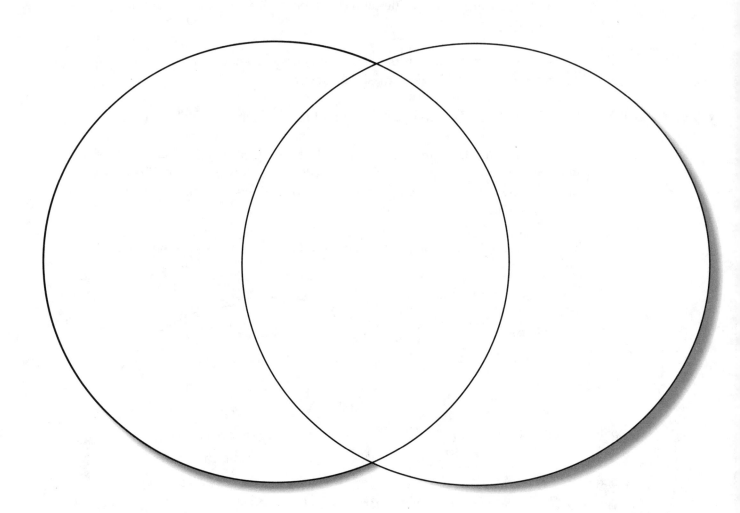

THESIS STATEMENT:

_____

_____

_____

Lesson 2 Organizing Information

Before you begin writing, you need to decide how you will organize your essay.

What to Do   Organize the details in the body of your essay in one of two ways.

You can arrange the details subject by subject. Using this plan, you write a paragraph that discusses all the features of one subject. Then you write a paragraph that discusses all the features of the second subject.

You can arrange the details feature by feature. In this plan, you write a paragraph that discusses the features of your two subjects one by one.

How to Do It   Jani made a comparison chart to see how both methods would work for her.

SUBJECT BY SUBJECT	FEATURE BY FEATURE

SUBJECT 1: Robert Cormier
  FEATURE 1: Place of Birth
    Massachusetts
  FEATURE 2: Awards
    American Library Association
  FEATURE 3: Best Known Work
    The Chocolate War
  FEATURE 4: Type of Work
    Novels
 	
SUBJECT 2: Shel Silverstein
  FEATURE 1: Place of Birth
    Illinois
  FEATURE 2: Awards
    American Library Association
    International Reading
    Association
  FEATURE 3: Best Known Work
    Where the Sidewalk Ends
  FEATURE 4: Type of Work
    Poetry
	FEATURE 1: Place of Birth
	  SUBJECT 1: Robert Cormier:
	    Massachusetts
	  SUBJECT 2: Shel Silverstein:
	    Illinois
	FEATURE 2: Awards
	  SUBJECT 1: Robert Cormier:
	    American Library Association
	  SUBJECT 2: Shel Silverstein:
	    American Library Association
	    International Reading
	    Association
	FEATURE 3: Best Known Work
	  SUBJECT 1: Robert Cormier:
	    The Chocolate War
	  SUBJECT 2: Shel Silverstein:
	    Where the Sidewalk Ends
	FEATURE 4: Type of Work
	  SUBJECT 1: Robert Cormier:
	    Novels
	  SUBJECT 2: Shel Silverstein:
	    Poetry

Apply It   ▶ Try both organizations for your essay. Use a separate piece of paper to make a comparison chart like Jani's. List details from your Venn diagram. Decide which plan will work best for you.

Lesson 3 Drafting Your Essay

You have gathered your information and decided on the best organization for your essay. Now it is time to write your draft.

What to Do   On a separate sheet of paper, write a draft of your comparison and contrast. Use the details in your Venn diagram and comparison chart. Give your essay an introduction. Make comparisons and show contrasts in the body. Then conclude your essay.

How to Do It   Follow the steps in this checklist.

Draft the Introduction
☐ Begin with a sentence that will grab your readers' interest.
- Look at the draft of your thesis statement on page 56.
- Write a sentence or question about the thesis.
☐ Mention the two topics that you will compare and contrast.
☐ State your thesis.

Draft the Body
☐ Use your notes from the Venn diagram on page 56 and the comparison chart on page 57.
☐ Use the method of organization you chose after making the comparison chart.
☐ Follow the organization on the chart.
- If you chose to organize subject by subject, give each *subject* a paragraph of its own.
- If you chose to organize feature by feature, give each *feature* a paragraph of its own.
☐ Use transitional words and phrases to make the organization clear. Look at the charts on pages 14 and 30.

Draft the Conclusion
☐ Sum up the comparison and contrast that you have made.
- Write a sentence about an important similarity between the topics.
- Write another sentence about an important difference between the topics.
☐ Restate your thesis.

Apply It   ▶ On a separate sheet of paper, draft your comparison-and-contrast essay. Use the notes and plans you have made as you write. Do not worry about spelling and grammar right now. Get your ideas down on paper.

Lesson 4   Completing Your Essay

Give your essay the final touches that it needs to make it the best it can be. Remember that a comparison-and-contrast essay points out similarities and differences between two subjects.

What to Do

After you have written the draft, read it. Then revise it. When you have revised your draft, proofread it. Fix any mistakes in spelling, capitalization, punctuation, and grammar.

How to Do It

Use the revision checklist on page 35 and the one below, which focuses on key elements of a comparison-and-contrast essay. Use the proofreading checklist on page 36 and the one below, which lists problems to be especially careful about in a comparison-and-contrast essay.

Revision Checklist
- ☐ Grab your readers' interest. If you have not, add a sentence that does.
- ☐ Name the two subjects you will compare and contrast. If you have not, add a sentence now.
- ☐ State a thesis about the subjects. If you have not, add a thesis statement now.
- ☐ Follow one clear organization in the body. If you have not, rearrange the details now.
- ☐ Show your readers how the subjects are alike and different. If you need more examples, add them now.
- ☐ Use transitional words and phrases, such as *both, like,* and *on the other hand*. If you have not, add them now.
- ☐ In the conclusion, sum up the comparison and contrast. If you have not, add a summary sentence or two now.
- ☐ Restate your thesis. If you have not, do it now.

Proofreading Checklist
- ☐ Capitalize the first letter in each proper noun.
- ☐ Check the guide to grammar, mechanics, and usage on pages 76–80.

Apply It

▶ Make the changes that you think will improve your comparison and contrast. If you can, work with a partner. Help each other revise and proofread. Make a clean copy of your essay.

What Have You Learned in Unit 3?

Use these questions to gather and review your thoughts about the writing you did in Unit 3. Don't worry about writing complete sentences. Just put some thoughts, ideas, and reactions down for each question.

Summary of a Story

1. How do you introduce a summary of a story?

_____

2. What is included in the body of a summary of a story?

_____

3. What should you include in the conclusion of a summary of a story?

_____

How-to Explanation

4. What is the purpose of a how-to explanation?

_____

5. What do you need to know about your audience for a how-to explanation?

_____

6. What kinds of details are important in a how-to explanation?

_____

7. Why is it important for the directions in a how-to explanation to be in chronological order?

_____

Comparison-and-Contrast Essay

8. How can you decide if two subjects will be good to compare and contrast?

_____

9. What is a good way to select details for a comparison-and-contrast essay?

_____

10. What are two ways to organize a comparison-and-contrast essay?

_____

▶ If you can, share your answers with a partner or group. Talk about problems and successes you had while writing. Develop a group list of tips for each kind of writing you did in this unit.

UNIT 4 Writing on Assignment

Sometimes you will be told what to write. You will be given an assignment. This is true of adult writers, too. In all types of careers, people have writing to do as part of their jobs. Often, their writing assignments have deadlines. A deadline is the time when a writing project must be completed. To meet a deadline, you may have to shorten some of the writing steps.

What to Do   Become familiar with the two different kinds of exposition that you will write in this unit:

A Test Essay
A Research Paper

How to Do It   Learn the key elements of each kind of essay that you will write.

A test essay is unique in two important ways.

First, it is written in response to a question or a set of directions. You have to make sure that you answer the question or follow the directions.

Second, a test essay is written under a deadline. You must work as quickly and efficiently as possible. You must organize your thoughts as quickly as possible. You must limit your answer to what you can write before the deadline. You will not have much time to revise. You will be able to make only the most important changes.

The basic purpose of a research paper is to inform. Readers of research papers are looking for information. They expect to have a better understanding of a topic after reading a research paper.

The writer must do research, gather information, organize that information, and develop ideas that inform readers. Doing your research and organizing information about your topic are especially important steps.

Apply It   ▶ Find examples of each of the types of exposition you will write in this unit. Look for essays based on research in newspapers, magazines, and journals. Look for an essay that you have written for a test. If you can, work with a group to discuss how the writers of the examples (including you) have informed their audiences. Save the examples in your notebook.

CHAPTER 1 Writing a Test Essay

Many tests in English, social studies, and science classes include essays. Often, a test will ask you to read a statement and a series of questions. Then you will have to write an informative essay to answer the questions. Your teacher will expect you to provide facts and ideas about your topic.

What to Do

Learn what is unique about a test essay. A test essay is a short piece of writing that informs readers about a topic. It explains, analyzes causes and effects, and supports ideas with reasons and facts. Most often, it is written in response to a prompt. A prompt is a question or a set of directions. Here is a sample test prompt.

> When volcanoes erupt, they may cause great damage. In 1980, Mount St. Helens in the state of Washington erupted. On June 15, 1991, Mount Pinatubo in the Philippines erupted.
>
> Write a short essay to answer these questions about volcanoes: What is a volcano? How does a volcano form? What makes a volcano erupt?

How to Do It

Study this example. It is a part of a test essay that a student named Renaldo wrote in response to the test prompt.

> A volcano is an opening in the surface of the earth. This opening reaches deep inside, where hot liquid rock is under great pressure. When a volcano erupts, lava, hot gases, and rocks are blasted into the sky. A volcanic eruption is a violent, powerful event.
>
> A volcano forms when rocks melt deep inside the earth. This melted rock is called magma. When the rocks melt, they also produce a gas. This gas mixes with the magma and rises to the surface. There, the heat from the magma melts a big hole in the rock around it. This hole is called the magma chamber.

Review It   **1.** In which paragraph does Renaldo tell what a volcano is?

_____

2. The second question in the prompt is "How does a volcano form?" Which sentence in Renaldo's second paragraph shows that he will answer that question?

_____

_____

▶ Read the rest of Renaldo's test essay. Then follow the directions below it.

> A volcano erupts because pressure inside the chamber forces the magma up. The magma rises through a crack in the rock and makes a channel. If the pressure is great enough, the channel breaks open. This opening is called a vent.
>
> The gas and magma can rush through the channel and out the vent very quickly. That upward rush of gas and magma causes the volcanic eruption.

3. The third question in the prompt is "What makes a volcano erupt?" Which sentence above shows that he will answer that question?

_____

_____

4. Which sentence above explains why volcanic eruptions occur?

_____

_____

Lesson 1　Understanding the Prompt

Most test essays have to be planned and written quickly. You have only a certain amount of time before the test period is over. Therefore, you must organize your thoughts as quickly as possible.

What to Do　The first step in writing a great test essay is to focus on the prompt. Decide exactly what it asks you to do or tells you to do. Those are your reasons for writing.

How to Do It　Study the prompt from Renaldo's essay test. Note the key words that he underlined.

> When volcanoes erupt, they may cause great damage. In 1980, Mount St. Helens in the state of Washington erupted. On June 15, 1991, Mount Pinatubo in the Philippines erupted.
>
> Write a short essay to answer these questions about volcanoes: <u>What is</u> a volcano? <u>How does</u> a volcano form? <u>What makes</u> a volcano erupt?

Renaldo analyzed the prompt to understand the assignment. He found the key words *what is, how does,* and *what makes.* These words showed him that the prompt was telling him to do three things:

1. Explain what a volcano is.
2. Explain how a volcano forms.
3. Explain why a volcano erupts.

Review It　▶ Read this prompt. Underline key words and phrases that tell what the purpose for writing is.

> People have been interested in solar eclipses for thousands of years. What is a solar eclipse? What causes it? Why are people warned not to look directly at a solar eclipse? Write an essay that answers these questions.

Lesson 2 Organizing Your Thoughts Quickly

When you answer a test prompt, you must limit your answer to what you can cover in a few paragraphs. You do not have much time, so you have to get organized quickly.

What to Do   Use the prompt as a guide for your answer. List the key steps in answering the prompt.

How to Do It   Study this example. These are some notes that Renaldo made for the question about how a volcano forms. He wrote the notes quickly, as he thought of them. He knew that they were out of order. He just wanted to get them all jotted down. After he had made the notes, he numbered them to show the correct order.

> 3 magma rises up through a crack
>
> 4 makes a channel and vent
>
> 1 pressure builds in magma chamber
>
> 2 forces the magma upward
>
> 5 gas and magma rush through channel and out vent

When he wrote his essay, Renaldo followed the numbers and used transitions to make a clear paragraph.

Apply It   ▶ Look back at the test prompt that you analyzed in Review It on page 64. Find information about it in an encyclopedia or science textbook. On the lines below, quickly jot notes. Then number them to show the correct order. Give yourself a time limit of 5 to 10 minutes.

_____

_____

_____

_____

_____

_____

_____

Lesson 3 Drafting Under a Deadline

A deadline is a writer's term for the date or time when a writing project must be completed. To meet a deadline, you may have to shorten some of the writing steps.

What to Do   Adjust to the deadline. When you are writing a test essay, you are writing under a deadline. You may have only thirty minutes to an hour to complete your essay. Therefore, you must work as quickly and efficiently as possible.

How to Do It   These tips will help you to get organized and draft your test essay.

Organizing
- Quickly organize your notes into a list or an outline. Look it over. Make sure that it is clear and complete.

- To make a cause-effect chain quickly, number your notes in the correct order.

Drafting
- Do not let the time pressure get to you. Relax. You have analyzed the prompt and made complete notes. The most difficult part of the writing assignment is actually over.

- Write or print as neatly as possible. Because this is a test, you probably will not be able to make a fresh, final copy of your essay.

- Skip a line between lines of writing. This will leave you space to make revisions and proofreading changes once your draft is complete.

- Follow these steps to complete your draft as quickly as possible. Refer to your notes as you write.

  - Introduction
    If the prompt asks you to make a general statement about the topic, do it here.
    If no general statement is needed, introduce the topic in one sentence.

  - Body
    Respond to each question or direction in an individual paragraph.
    Use facts, details, and examples to explain each statement you make.
    Organize your paragraphs logically.
    Write in complete sentences.

  - Conclusion
    End with a short statement about the overall topic.

Apply It

▶ Use one of the following test prompts to practice planning and drafting your test essay. If you wish, set a time limit for yourself so that you can practice writing under a deadline. Allow yourself thirty minutes in total to answer the question. Spend 5 to 10 minutes planning and organizing. Spend about 15 minutes writing the draft. Allow 5 to 10 minutes to revise and proofread in Lesson 4.

▶ First, read the prompts and choose one.

1. People have been interested in solar eclipses for thousands of years. What is a solar eclipse? What causes it? Why are people warned not to look directly at a solar eclipse? Write an essay that answers these questions.

2. People who live along the Pacific Ocean in California, South America, and Asia have something in common. They all live in areas that are prone to earthquakes. Write an essay about earthquakes. Explain what causes them and what their effects are.

▶ On a separate sheet of paper, jot notes and organize them. Finally, begin a draft of your answer below. Continue on a separate sheet of paper, if necessary.

_____

_____

_____

_____

_____

_____

_____

Lesson 4 Completing a Test Essay

You will not have time to make all the changes you would like to make. Make the ones that affect the meaning of your work first. Those are the most important ones.

What to Do   Finish the draft of your essay before your time is up. You want to have enough time to go over it quickly.

How to Do It   Because you are taking a test, you will not be able to revise and proofread with a partner. Make any changes that you think will improve your test essay. Write or print as neatly as possible. Make it clear where words and phrases should be inserted. Rely on your own good judgment, and use these checklists for help.

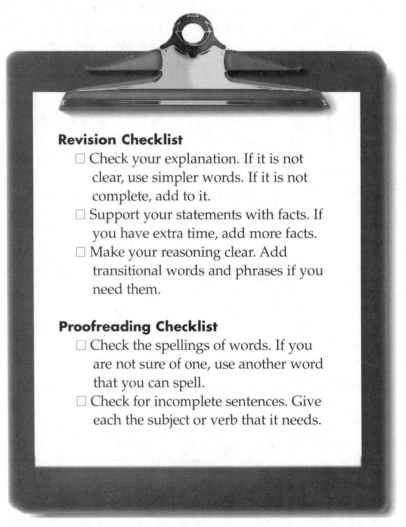

Revision Checklist
- ☐ Check your explanation. If it is not clear, use simpler words. If it is not complete, add to it.
- ☐ Support your statements with facts. If you have extra time, add more facts.
- ☐ Make your reasoning clear. Add transitional words and phrases if you need them.

Proofreading Checklist
- ☐ Check the spellings of words. If you are not sure of one, use another word that you can spell.
- ☐ Check for incomplete sentences. Give each the subject or verb that it needs.

Apply It   ▶ Revise and proofread the draft of your test essay. Work right on the draft you started on page 67. Make the changes as neatly as you can.

▶ If this had been a real test, you would now turn your paper in to be graded. If you can, meet with a small group of students. Share your test essays. Discuss the process of writing a test essay. Help one another to relax regarding test essays. Give one another suggestions for improving them.

CHAPTER 2 Writing a Research Report

Teachers often assign research reports. A research report is a careful examination of a topic. A research report can give new information on a familiar topic.

What to Do
Learn the key elements of a research report. A research report

- gives facts and information about a topic that interests the writer.
- presents a thesis statement and gives details to support it.
- has an introduction, body, and conclusion.
- collects information from many different sources.
- gives the sources of the information, ideas, and material used.

How to Do It
Look at this example. A student named Tony decided to write a report on the names of his classmates. His introduction tells what will follow. It also shows how interested he is in his topic.

"What's in a name?"[1] William Shakespeare asked that question in his play Romeo and Juliet. In this report, I will answer that question about the names of the students in my English class. I will explore where our names come from, what they mean, and how we ended up with them. I will tell some interesting stories about our nicknames. I will list a few people, famous and not-so famous, who share our names.

"What's in a name?" Well, as my uncle said, "My name is the most precious thing I have. It belongs only to me. Yet it carries the history of me, my parents, their parents, and their parents before them."[2]

1. William Shakespeare, Romeo and Juliet, Act II, scene ii, line 43
2. Interview with Franco Martinez, recorded April 17, 1995

Apply It
▶ In this chapter, you will write a research report about names. For this project, you might work alone, with a partner, or with a small group. Brainstorm with your classmates ways to begin your report on names.

Lesson 1 Gathering Information

One of the most important steps in writing a report is gathering information, or doing research. When you research a topic, you find what sources are available. Then you decide which sources to use.

What to Do   Find out about available resources. Remember that this is the age of information. You may not realize how many sources of information surround you.

How to Do It   Study this list that Tony made for himself. These are the sources he planned to use.

> Go to the library to find:
>
> encyclopedia articles on names
>
> books on names
>
> magazine articles on names
>
> Talk to parents, grandparents, and other relatives.
>
> Search the Internet and on-line services.
>
> Post questions about names on computer bulletin boards.

Before you begin to research, make a list of questions about your topic. Here are some questions that Tony came up with during a group discussion.

> QUESTIONS TO ANSWER
>
> What is the history of our last names?
>
> How did our parents choose our first names?
>
> Does the name have a specific meaning?
>
> Does the name come from a place, an occupation, or an event?
>
> What famous people had this name?
>
> What are the ethnic origins of our names?
>
> How is the American spelling different from the original?
>
> What nicknames come from our first and last names?

Apply It   ▶ On a separate sheet of paper, write a list of sources that you can use. Then write a list of questions you want to answer in your report. Keep these lists with you as you do your research.

Lesson 2 Taking Notes

Taking good notes will help you write your report.

What to Do   Learn how to take good notes. Here are a few useful tips.

- Write neatly. Notes are only useful if you can read them later.
- Use a separate page or card for each note.
- Include as many details as possible. Do not leave out important facts.
- Keep notes organized. Mark them so that you can put them back in order if they get mixed up. One good way is to put the research question at the top of the page or card.
- Put information you find in your own words. Enclose what information you copy word for word in quotation marks. Be exact when you copy a passage.
- Write the source for each fact, detail, or quoted passage. Be sure the source information is correct.

How to Do It   Here are some notes that Tony made.

What nicknames come from our first names?	
First Names	Nicknames
Anthony	Tony
Elizabeth	Beth, Liz, Betty, Liza
Enrique	Rico, Ricky
Consuela	Connie
Michelle	Shelly
_____	
Gilbert, Martha. <u>Names and Nicknames.</u> New York: Personal Press, 1993.	

Apply It   ▶ Write each question that you want answered on a separate note card or page of your notebook. Then do your research. Write your notes on the information you find for each question.

Lesson 3   Organizing Your Report

You have collected the information you need. Now is the time to organize your notes and create an outline.

What to Do   Make a plan for presenting your information. First, come up with a one-sentence thesis statement that tells the main idea of your report. Then sort your notes and make an outline.

How to Do It   Tony came up with this thesis statement for his report.

> The histories and meanings of our names show why America has been called the "melting pot of the world."

Then Tony sorted his notes and wrote this outline.

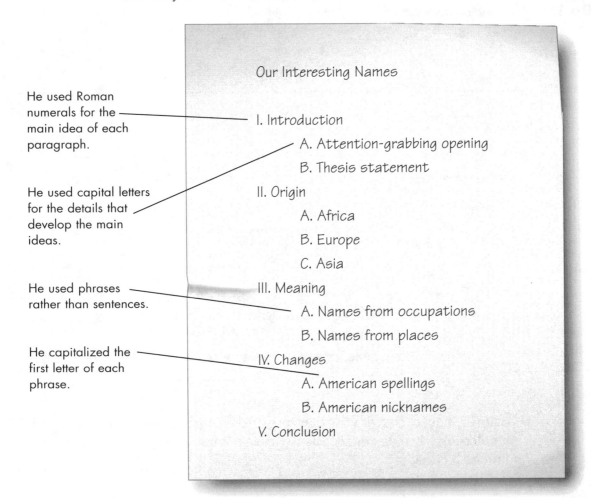

He used Roman numerals for the main idea of each paragraph.

He used capital letters for the details that develop the main ideas.

He used phrases rather than sentences.

He capitalized the first letter of each phrase.

Our Interesting Names

I. Introduction
    A. Attention-grabbing opening
    B. Thesis statement
II. Origin
    A. Africa
    B. Europe
    C. Asia
III. Meaning
    A. Names from occupations
    B. Names from places
IV. Changes
    A. American spellings
    B. American nicknames
V. Conclusion

Apply It   ▶ First, write a thesis statement for your report. Then make an outline from your notes. Keep the outline simple. This will make it easier for you to follow when you write the report.

Lesson 4 Writing Your Report

You have done your research. Your notes are organized. Now it is time to write a draft of your report.

What to Do Write a draft of your report. Make sure your report has an introduction, a body, and a conclusion. After you have written the draft, read it. Then revise it and proofread it.

How to Do It Use your notes and outline to draft your report. Then use the revision checklist on page 35 and the one below, which focuses on key elements of a research report. Use the proofreading checklist on page 36 and the one below, which lists problems to be especially careful about in a research report.

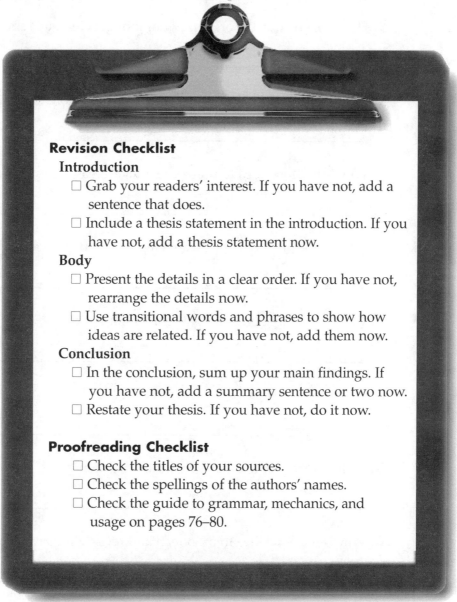

Revision Checklist

Introduction
- ☐ Grab your readers' interest. If you have not, add a sentence that does.
- ☐ Include a thesis statement in the introduction. If you have not, add a thesis statement now.

Body
- ☐ Present the details in a clear order. If you have not, rearrange the details now.
- ☐ Use transitional words and phrases to show how ideas are related. If you have not, add them now.

Conclusion
- ☐ In the conclusion, sum up your main findings. If you have not, add a summary sentence or two now.
- ☐ Restate your thesis. If you have not, do it now.

Proofreading Checklist
- ☐ Check the titles of your sources.
- ☐ Check the spellings of the authors' names.
- ☐ Check the guide to grammar, mechanics, and usage on pages 76–80.

Apply It ▶ Use your note cards and your outline to write a draft of your report. After you have written your draft, revise it. Then proofread it and correct any mistakes. If you can, get together with other students and brainstorm ways to publish your reports.

What Have You Learned in Unit 4?

Use these questions to gather and review your thoughts about the writing you did in Unit 4. Don't worry about writing complete sentences. Just put some thoughts, ideas, and reactions down for each question.

Test Essay

1. What is a test essay prompt?

_____

2. What should you look for in a test essay prompt?

_____

3. How can you quickly organize your thoughts for a test essay?

_____

4. Why should you stop drafting a few minutes before the deadline?

_____

5. Why is it a good idea to use your strongest reason first in a test essay?

_____

Research Report

6. What is the purpose of a research report?

_____

7. What are some sources for gathering information?

_____

8. What are some tips for good note taking?

_____

9. Why is it helpful to organize your information?

_____

10. Why is it a good idea to proofread and revise a research report?

_____

▶ If you can, share your answers with a partner or group. Talk about the writing experiences you had. Share problems and successes. Develop a list of tips for each kind of writing you did in this unit.

The Writing Process

The writing process
What happens when a writer turns words into a story or an essay? He or she follows a set of steps, from start to finish. These steps make up the writing process. If you follow the same steps, you can make the process work for you.

What is a process?
A process is a series of steps that lead to a goal. Each step brings the process closer to the goal. Suppose you wanted to grow a pepper plant in a pot. Growing a plant is a process. You choose seeds, plant them, water the plants, and pull weeds. Each step gets you closer to your goal, and finally you pick the peppers.

What is the writing process?
There are five main steps in the writing process. They are prewriting, drafting, revising, proofreading, and publishing. This chart shows them. You won't always follow them in order, and you may move back and forth between stages.

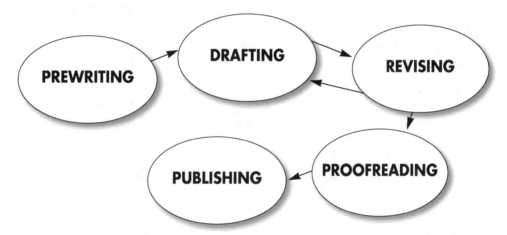

Prewriting
In prewriting, you decide what to write. This step is like deciding what seeds to grow. You explore your idea. You think about it and gather information about it. You organize your ideas. You think about the people you will be writing for. You decide what they need to know and how you want to tell it to them.

Drafting
In drafting, you put your ideas into words. You shape your words into sentences. You build your sentences into paragraphs. As you draft, you do not have to worry about parts that are not quite right. You will fix them in the next stage.

Revising
In revising, you improve your draft. You look for weak spots, such as a word that is not quite right. You make changes, or revisions, to strengthen those spots. Notice that the arrows in the drafting and revising sections can lead you back and forth. This part of the process is like watering and weeding in the growing process.

Proofreading
When you are satisfied with your revised work, you turn to proofreading. This stage is sometimes called editing. In this step, you check for and correct any errors you may have made in grammar, usage, and mechanics, including spelling.

Publishing
Finally, in the publishing stage, you make a final copy and publish it or share it with an audience.

GRAMMAR

Nouns A **noun** is the name of a person, place, or thing. A **common noun** names any person, place, or thing. A **proper noun** names a particular person, place, or thing.

Common Nouns	Proper Nouns
ballplayer	Cal Ripken
city	Los Angeles
river	Hudson River
country	Peru
street	Jackson Avenue

Pronouns Pronouns are words that stand for or take the place of nouns.
The subject pronouns are:

Singular	Plural
I	we
you	you
he	they
she	they
it	they

Use a **subject pronoun** as the subject of a sentence.

Incorrect
Her and Rosa will be here soon.
Revision
She and Rosa will be here soon.

Use **subject pronouns** after the linking verb *to be*.

Incorrect
The winners were Leroy and him.
Revision
The winners were Leroy and he.

The object pronouns are:

Singular	Plural
me	us
you	you
him	them
her	them
it	them

Use **object pronouns** as the direct objects of sentences. A direct object receives the action in a sentence.

Incorrect
Rosa will call Leo and I.
Revision
Rosa will call Leo and me.

Use object pronouns as objects of prepositions. The object of a preposition is a noun or pronoun at the end of a prepositional phrase. (See **Prepositions**.)

Incorrect
Selena wrote to Duane and I.
Revision
Selena wrote to Duane and me.

Possessive pronouns show ownership. The possessive pronouns are:

Singular	Plural
my	our
your	your
his	their
her	their
its	their

Verbs A **verb** is a word that shows action or the fact that something exists. Verbs change form to show time. These forms are called *tenses*.

Use **irregular verbs** correctly. Some verbs have unusual forms for showing that an action happened in the past. When in doubt, check a dictionary or ask a good editor (such as your teacher).

Incorrect
The group sung their hits.
Revision
The group sang their hits.

Adjectives An **adjective** is a word used to describe a noun or pronoun. A **proper adjective** is made from a proper noun. It names a particular person, place, or thing.

Use the correct form to compare adjectives. To compare two persons, places, or things, use the **comparative** form. Add *-er* to most short adjectives. Use *more* with longer adjectives. Use one or the other, not both.

Incorrect	Revision
more long movie	longer movie
thrillinger movie	more thrilling movie
more newer movie	newer movie

To compare more than two persons, places, or things, use the **superlative** form. Add -*est* to most short adjectives. Use *most* with longer adjectives. Use one or the other, not both.

Incorrect	Revision
most slow bus	slowest bus
comfortablest bus	most comfortable bus
most noisiest bus	noisiest bus

Some adjectives use different words for comparisons.

Examples

bad	worse	worst
good	better	best

Adverbs
An **adverb** is a word that modifies a verb, an adjective, or another adverb.

Do not use an adjective when you need an adverb.

Incorrect	Revision
We did the job good.	We did the job well.
We did it quick.	We did it quickly.

Use the correct form to compare adverbs. To compare two actions, use the **comparative form**. Add -*er* to most short adverbs. Use *more* with most adverbs. Use one or the other, not both.

Incorrect	Revision
spoke more softlier	spoke more softly
started more later	started later

To compare more than two actions, use the **superlative form**. 1. Use -*est* with some short adverbs. 2. Use *most* with most adverbs. 3. Use one or the other, not both.

Incorrect	Revision
spoke most softliest	spoke most softly
started most latest	started latest

Some adverbs use different words for comparisons.

Examples

badly	worse	worst
well	better	best

Prepositions
A **preposition** is a word that relates the noun or pronoun following it to another word in the sentence.

Examples

in	on	off	of	under
over	along	beside	above	between

I saw the funnel of a tornado in the distance. The funnel was moving in my direction.

Sentences
A **sentence** is a group of words with two main parts: a complete subject and a complete predicate. Together these parts express a complete thought.

Use complete sentences, not **fragments**. A complete sentence has a subject and a verb. A fragment is missing one of those parts. Correct a fragment by adding the missing part.

Fragment
The book written by Gary Soto.
Revision
The book was written by Gary Soto.
Fragment
Because the rain finally stopped.
Revision
We went out because the rain finally stopped.

Avoid **run-on sentences**. A run-on sentence is really more than one sentence. Correct a run-on sentence by dividing it into two (or more) sentences.

Run-on
For months I saved all the money I earned, and I never spent any of it, and finally I had enough for the class trip.
Revision
For months I saved all the money I earned. I never spent any of it. Finally I had enough for the class trip.

Subject-Verb Agreement
Make the subject and verb of a sentence agree in number. To make a subject and verb agree, make sure that both are **singular** or both are **plural**. A singular subject names one person, place,

or thing. A plural subject names more than one person, place, or thing.

Incorrect
Some parts is missing.
Revision
Some parts are missing.

Be careful when a **prepositional phrase** comes between the subject and the verb. The verb must agree with the subject, not with the object of the preposition.

Incorrect
One of the parts are missing.
Revision
One of the parts is missing.

The pronoun *I* is singular, but it nearly always takes the plural form of a verb. (The only exceptions are *am* and *was*, which are singular forms of the verb *to be*.)

Incorrect
I urges you to act now.
Revision
I urge you to act now.
Incorrect
I is nearly ready.
Revision
I am nearly ready.

Phrases A **phrase** is a group of words, without a subject and verb, that works in a sentence as one part of speech.

A **prepositional phrase** is a group of words that includes a **preposition** and the **object of the preposition**, a noun or pronoun. The whole phrase works like an adjective or adverb. It modifies the meaning of another word or group of words.

Keep prepositions and their phrases close to the words they modify. Your sentence may not say what you mean if a prepositional phrase is in the wrong place.

One Meaning
The car with stripes looks great.
(but another car does not)
Another Meaning
The car looks great with stripes.
(but not without stripes)

Negatives A **negative** is a word or word part

that means "not." The word *not* itself is a negative. So are *nobody* and *nowhere*. The contraction *-n't* is made from *not*. When *-n't* is part of a word, it is a negative.

Use only one negative in a sentence. More than one negative in a sentence is a "double negative." Remove double negatives in your sentences.

Incorrect
We don't have no blank cassettes.
Revision
We don't have any blank cassettes.
We have no blank cassettes.

MECHANICS

Capitalization Capitalize the first word of a sentence.

Incorrect
the sun looked like an orange.
Revision
The sun looked like an orange.

Capitalize proper nouns.

Incorrect	**Revision**
boston red sox	Boston Red Sox
ernesto galarza	Ernesto Galarza
thailand	Thailand

Capitalize proper adjectives.

Incorrect
foreign and american cars
Revision
foreign and American cars

Capitalize the first word and all important words in titles of books, movies, and other works of art.

Incorrect	**Revision**
Jurassic park	*Jurassic Park*

Capitalize a person's title when it is followed by the person's name.

Incorrect	**Revision**
senator Marston	Senator Marston

Punctuation

End Marks Use an end mark at the end of

every sentence. Use a period to end a sentence that makes a statement or gives a command. Use a question mark to end a question. Use an exclamation point after a statement showing strong emotion.

Incorrect
This is the movie to see
Have you seen it already
Yes, and it's great

Revisions
This is the movie to see.
Have you seen it already?
Yes, and it's great!

Commas
Use a comma between the two independent clauses in a compound sentence.

Incorrect
Levon was standing in the doorway and his brother was sitting on the sofa.

Revision
Levon was standing in the doorway, and his brother was sitting on the sofa.

Use commas to separate three or more words in a series.

Incorrect
I bought a shirt a cap and a compact disc.

Revision
I bought a shirt, a cap, and a compact disc.

Use commas to set the rest of the sentence apart from the spoken words in a direct quotation.

Incorrect
She said "I'm not ready."
"Wait here" he said "until I return."

Revision
She said, "I'm not ready."
"Wait here," he said, "until I return."

Quotation Marks
A direct quotation represents a person's exact words. Use quotation marks around the words the speaker says.

Incorrect
Mr. Hsu said, Take tomorrow off.

Revision
Mr. Hsu said, "Take tomorrow off."

When you use a comma or a period with a direct quotation, place it inside the final quotation mark.

Incorrect
"I'll see you tomorrow", I said.
She said, "I'll be waiting".

Revision
"I'll see you tomorrow," I said.
She said, "I'll be waiting."

When you use a question mark or exclamation point with a direct quotation, place it inside the quotation marks if it goes with the speaker's words.

Incorrect
I called, "Is anybody home"?
A voice answered, "I'll be right there"!

Revision
I called, "Is anybody home?"
A voice answered, "I'll be right there!"

Dialogue is written conversation. When you write dialogue, start a new paragraph each time the speaker changes. Begin a new paragraph each time a different person speaks.

Incorrect
"Good morning," he said. "Says who?" I answered.

Revision
"Good morning," he said.
"Says who?" I answered.

Apostrophes
A possessive noun shows ownership, as *Luis's* does in *Luis's dog*. To make a singular noun possessive, add an apostrophe (') and an *s*, no matter what letter ends the noun.

Noun	Possessive
student	student's
boss	boss's

To make a plural noun possessive, add an apostrophe and an *s* if the noun ends with some letter other than *s*. Add only an apostrophe if the noun ends with *s*.

Noun	Possessive
children	children's
students	students'
families	families'
lawyers	lawyers'

Possessive pronouns show ownership, like possessive nouns. However, possessive pronouns are not spelled with apostrophes.

Incorrect
Those snapshots are their's.
The dog ate it's food.
Revision
Those snapshots are theirs.
The dog ate its food.

USAGE

bad, badly Use *bad* after linking verbs, such as *feel*, *look*, and *seem*. Use *badly* whenever an adverb is needed.

Incorrect
I felt badly about not being able to play in the game.
Revision
I felt bad about not being able to play in the game.

beside, besides Do not confuse these two prepositions, which have different meanings. Beside means "at the side of" or "close to." Besides means "in addition to."

Incorrect
I wondered whether anyone would be going on the trip beside the usual group.
Revision
I wondered whether anyone would be going on the trip besides the usual group.

can, may The verb *can* generally refers to the ability to do something. The verb *may* generally refers to permission to do something.

Incorrect
"Can I have the last hamburger?" he asked.
Revision
"May I have the last hamburger?" he asked.

good, well Use the predicate adjective *good* after linking verbs, such as *feel*, *look*, *smell*, *taste*, and *seem*. Use *well* whenever you need an adverb.

Incorrect
We hadn't won the game, but we could hold our heads high because we knew that we played good.
Revision
We hadn't won the game, but we could hold our heads high because we knew that we played well.

its, it's Do not confuse the possessive pronoun *its* with the contraction *it's*, standing for *it is* or *it has*.

Incorrect
That dog has something stuck in it's paw.
Revision
That dog has something stuck in its paw.

of, have Do not use *of* in place of *have* after auxiliary verbs, such as *would*, *could*, *should*, *may*, *might*, or *must*.

Incorrect
You should of seen the way Hakeem went up for the rebound.
Revision
You should have seen the way Hakeem went up for the rebound.

than, then The conjunction *than* is used to connect the two parts of a comparison. Do not confuse *than* with the adverb *then*, which usually refers to time.

Incorrect
My brother is exactly a year older then I am.
Revision
My brother is exactly a year older than I am.

their, there, they're Do not confuse the spellings of these three words. *Their* is a possessive pronoun and always modifies a noun. *There* is usually used either at the beginning of a sentence or as an adverb. *They're* is a contraction for *they are*.

Incorrect
"Are those they're sweat pants?" I asked. "No," he said. "There over their, behind the lockers."
Revision
"Are those their sweat pants?" I asked. "No," he said. "They're over there, behind the lockers."